50 Eastern Comfort Recipes for Home

By: Kelly Johnson

Table of Contents

- Spicy Lamb Kebabs
- Pomegranate Chicken
- Persian Herb Rice
- Stuffed Grape Leaves
- Middle Eastern Spiced Chickpeas
- Sumac Roasted Chicken
- Lentil Soup with Lemon
- Falafel with Tahini Sauce
- Shawarma Beef Wraps
- Baba Ganoush
- Roasted Eggplant Salad
- Moroccan Tagine with Apricots
- Stuffed Bell Peppers
- Hummus with Pine Nuts
- Grilled Kofta
- Saffron Rice with Raisins
- Harissa-Spiced Carrots
- Chicken with Olives and Preserved Lemons
- Tabbouleh Salad
- Mujadara (Lentil and Rice Pilaf)
- Fattoush Salad
- Yogurt-Marinated Chicken
- Moroccan Chickpea Stew
- Date and Nut Couscous
- Roasted Cauliflower with Cumin
- Chicken Shawarma Salad
- Moussaka
- Spiced Couscous with Dried Fruit
- Eggplant and Tomato Stew
- Lamb and Spinach Stew
- Greek Lemon Potatoes
- Za'atar Roasted Chicken
- Caramelized Onion Rice
- Persian Chicken Kebabs
- Lebanese Meat Pies
- Sautéed Spinach with Garlic

- Fennel and Orange Salad
- Moroccan Carrot Salad
- Almond and Honey Baklava
- Yogurt-Cucumber Dip
- Rosewater Rice Pudding
- Stuffed Acorn Squash
- Harira Soup
- Spiced Lamb Chops
- Eggplant and Chickpea Curry
- Lebanese Rice Pilaf
- Middle Eastern Chicken Stew
- Pita Bread with Za'atar
- Tahini-Sesame Noodles
- Sweet and Savory Date Bars

Spicy Lamb Kebabs

Ingredients:

For the Marinade:

- **2 tablespoons olive oil**
- **2 tablespoons lemon juice** (freshly squeezed)
- **4 cloves garlic**, minced
- **1 tablespoon ground cumin**
- **1 tablespoon ground paprika** (or smoked paprika for extra depth)
- **1 teaspoon ground coriander**
- **1 teaspoon ground turmeric**
- **1/2 teaspoon ground cinnamon**
- **1/2 teaspoon ground black pepper**
- **1/2 teaspoon cayenne pepper** (adjust to taste for spiciness)
- **1 teaspoon salt**
- **1 tablespoon fresh rosemary** (or 1 teaspoon dried rosemary), chopped
- **1 tablespoon fresh mint** (or 1 teaspoon dried mint), chopped
- **1 pound lamb shoulder or lamb leg**, trimmed and cut into 1-inch cubes

For the Kebabs:

- **1 large onion**, cut into chunks
- **1 red bell pepper**, cut into chunks
- **1 green bell pepper**, cut into chunks
- **1 zucchini**, sliced into thick rounds
- **Wooden or metal skewers**

Instructions:

1. Prepare the Marinade:

1. **Combine Ingredients:** In a large bowl, mix together the olive oil, lemon juice, minced garlic, cumin, paprika, coriander, turmeric, cinnamon, black pepper, cayenne pepper, salt, rosemary, and mint.
2. **Marinate Lamb:** Add the lamb cubes to the bowl and toss to coat evenly. Cover and refrigerate for at least 1 hour, or up to overnight for maximum flavor.

2. Prepare the Kebabs:

1. **Preheat Grill:** Preheat your grill to medium-high heat. If using wooden skewers, soak them in water for at least 30 minutes to prevent burning.
2. **Assemble Kebabs:** Thread the marinated lamb cubes onto the skewers, alternating with chunks of onion, bell peppers, and zucchini.

3. **Grill Kebabs:** Place the skewers on the grill and cook for 10-12 minutes, turning occasionally, until the lamb is cooked to your desired level of doneness and has a nice char. The internal temperature for medium-rare lamb is about 145°F (63°C), and for medium it is 160°F (71°C).

3. Serve:

1. **Rest Lamb:** Allow the kebabs to rest for a few minutes after grilling to let the juices redistribute.
2. **Serve:** Serve the kebabs hot with your choice of sides. They pair well with rice, couscous, pita bread, and a fresh salad or yogurt sauce.

Tips:

- **Marinating:** For the best flavor, marinate the lamb for several hours or overnight.
- **Vegetables:** Feel free to use any vegetables you like or have on hand. Cherry tomatoes, mushrooms, or eggplant are also great additions.
- **Grill Temperature:** Make sure your grill is properly preheated for a good sear and to prevent sticking.

Enjoy your Spicy Lamb Kebabs—a vibrant and delicious dish with just the right amount of heat!

Pomegranate Chicken

Ingredients:

- **4 boneless, skinless chicken breasts** (or thighs, if preferred)
- **Salt and freshly ground black pepper**, to taste
- **2 tablespoons olive oil**
- **1 small onion**, finely chopped
- **3 cloves garlic**, minced
- **1 cup pomegranate juice**
- **1/4 cup balsamic vinegar**
- **1/4 cup honey** (or maple syrup)
- **1 tablespoon soy sauce**
- **1 teaspoon dried thyme** (or 1 tablespoon fresh thyme)
- **1 teaspoon ground cumin**
- **1/2 teaspoon ground paprika**
- **1/4 teaspoon red pepper flakes** (optional, for extra heat)
- **1 tablespoon cornstarch** (optional, for thickening)
- **2 tablespoons water** (if using cornstarch)
- **Fresh pomegranate seeds** (for garnish)
- **Chopped fresh parsley** (for garnish)

Instructions:

1. Prepare the Chicken:

1. **Season Chicken:** Season the chicken breasts with salt and black pepper on both sides.
2. **Sear Chicken:** Heat the olive oil in a large skillet over medium-high heat. Add the chicken breasts and cook for about 5-7 minutes per side, or until golden brown and cooked through. Remove from the skillet and set aside.

2. Make the Pomegranate Glaze:

1. **Sauté Aromatics:** In the same skillet, add the chopped onion and cook for 3-4 minutes, or until softened. Add the minced garlic and cook for an additional 1 minute.
2. **Add Liquids and Spices:** Pour in the pomegranate juice, balsamic vinegar, honey, soy sauce, thyme, cumin, paprika, and red pepper flakes (if using). Stir to combine and bring the mixture to a simmer.
3. **Reduce Sauce:** Allow the sauce to simmer for about 10-15 minutes, or until it reduces by about half and thickens. If you prefer a thicker sauce, mix the cornstarch with the water to create a slurry, then stir it into the sauce and cook for an additional 2-3 minutes until thickened.

3. Combine and Serve:

1. **Return Chicken:** Return the seared chicken breasts to the skillet and spoon the sauce over them. Simmer for an additional 5 minutes to allow the flavors to meld and the chicken to heat through.
2. **Garnish:** Remove from heat and garnish with fresh pomegranate seeds and chopped parsley.

4. Serve:

1. **Plate:** Serve the Pomegranate Chicken over rice, couscous, or with a side of steamed vegetables. Drizzle additional sauce over the chicken and side dishes if desired.

Tips:

- **Pomegranate Juice:** Use 100% pomegranate juice for the best flavor. Avoid cocktail blends with added sugars.
- **Thickening Sauce:** If you prefer a thicker glaze, the cornstarch slurry can help, but be sure to cook it for a few minutes to eliminate the raw cornstarch flavor.
- **Chicken Alternatives:** This recipe works well with chicken thighs or bone-in chicken pieces. Adjust cooking times accordingly.

Enjoy your Pomegranate Chicken—a flavorful and elegant dish that's sure to impress!

Persian Herb Rice

Ingredients:

- **2 cups basmati rice**
- **1/2 cup fresh dill**, chopped
- **1/2 cup fresh cilantro**, chopped
- **1/2 cup fresh parsley**, chopped
- **1/2 cup fresh chives** or green onions, chopped
- **1/2 teaspoon ground turmeric** (optional, for color)
- **1/4 teaspoon ground cinnamon** (optional, for additional flavor)
- **1/4 cup vegetable oil** or melted butter
- **1 teaspoon salt**
- **1/2 teaspoon black pepper**
- **1/2 teaspoon saffron threads** (optional, soaked in 2 tablespoons warm water)
- **1 large onion**, finely chopped (optional, for additional flavor)
- **2-3 cloves garlic**, minced (optional, for additional flavor)
- **Water** (for cooking rice)

Instructions:

1. Prepare the Rice:

1. **Rinse Rice:** Rinse the basmati rice under cold water until the water runs clear. This removes excess starch and helps prevent the rice from becoming gummy.
2. **Soak Rice:** Soak the rice in a large bowl of water for at least 30 minutes. This helps the rice grains cook more evenly.
3. **Cook Rice:** Drain the soaked rice and bring a large pot of water to a boil. Add a teaspoon of salt and the drained rice. Cook the rice for 5-7 minutes, or until the grains are slightly tender but still firm in the center. Drain the rice and set aside.

2. Prepare the Herb Mixture:

1. **Sauté Onion and Garlic (Optional):** If using, heat a tablespoon of oil or butter in a large skillet over medium heat. Add the chopped onion and cook until translucent. Add the minced garlic and cook for another minute. Remove from heat.
2. **Mix Herbs:** In a large bowl, combine the chopped dill, cilantro, parsley, and chives.

3. Assemble and Cook the Rice:

1. **Layering:** In a large, heavy-bottomed pot, heat the remaining oil or butter over medium heat. If using saffron, drizzle a little of the saffron water over the bottom of the pot. Add a layer of the partially cooked rice, then a layer of the herb mixture. Repeat the layers until all the rice and herbs are used, ending with a layer of rice on top.
2. **Steam the Rice:** Cover the pot with a tight-fitting lid. Reduce the heat to low and cook for about 30-40 minutes, allowing the rice to steam and the flavors to meld. If you want a

crispy bottom layer (tahdig), let the rice cook a bit longer and avoid stirring it during cooking.

4. Serve:

1. **Fluff Rice:** Gently fluff the rice with a fork before serving.
2. **Garnish (Optional):** Garnish with additional fresh herbs or a sprinkle of saffron if desired.

Tips:

- **Tahdig:** For the traditional crispy layer at the bottom, you can add a few tablespoons of yogurt mixed with a little flour to the bottom of the pot before layering the rice. This will create a crispy crust.
- **Herbs:** Fresh herbs are key to this dish's vibrant flavor. If fresh herbs aren't available, you can use dried herbs, but the flavor will be different.
- **Serving:** Persian Herb Rice is often served with grilled meats, stews, or yogurt. It's a versatile side that complements many dishes.

Enjoy your Persian Herb Rice—a fragrant and delicious accompaniment that brings a touch of Persian cuisine to your table!

Stuffed Grape Leaves

Ingredients:

For the Filling:

- **1 cup short-grain rice** (such as Arborio or sushi rice)
- **1/2 pound ground lamb** (or beef, if preferred)
- **1 large onion**, finely chopped
- **3 cloves garlic**, minced
- **1/4 cup pine nuts** (optional)
- **1/4 cup fresh dill**, chopped
- **1/4 cup fresh mint**, chopped
- **1/2 cup fresh parsley**, chopped
- **1/2 teaspoon ground cinnamon**
- **1/2 teaspoon ground cumin**
- **1/2 teaspoon ground allspice**
- **Salt and black pepper**, to taste
- **2 tablespoons olive oil**

For the Grape Leaves:

- **1 jar grape leaves** (about 16 ounces), packed in brine, rinsed and drained
- **1 lemon**, thinly sliced
- **1/2 cup olive oil** (for drizzling)

For Cooking:

- **1 cup water** (or chicken/vegetable broth)

Instructions:

1. Prepare the Filling:

1. **Cook Rice:** Rinse the rice under cold water until the water runs clear. Cook the rice in a small pot with 1 1/2 cups water, following package instructions but reducing the cooking time by about 5 minutes to keep it slightly undercooked. Drain and set aside.
2. **Cook Meat and Vegetables:** In a large skillet, heat 2 tablespoons olive oil over medium heat. Add the chopped onion and cook until softened, about 5 minutes. Add the minced garlic and cook for another minute.
3. **Add Meat and Nuts:** Add the ground lamb (or beef) to the skillet. Cook until browned, breaking it up with a spoon as it cooks. If using pine nuts, add them and cook for an additional 2 minutes.
4. **Combine Ingredients:** Add the cooked rice, dill, mint, parsley, cinnamon, cumin, allspice, salt, and black pepper to the meat mixture. Stir well to combine and cook for another 2-3 minutes. Remove from heat and let cool slightly.

2. Prepare the Grape Leaves:

1. **Prepare Leaves:** Carefully remove the grape leaves from the jar and rinse them under cold water to remove excess brine. If the leaves are large, you may want to trim the stems.

3. Stuff and Roll the Grape Leaves:

1. **Place Filling:** Lay a grape leaf flat on a work surface with the stem end facing you. Place about 1 tablespoon of the filling in the center of the leaf.
2. **Fold and Roll:** Fold the sides of the grape leaf over the filling, then roll from the stem end towards the tip to form a tight, compact roll. Repeat with the remaining leaves and filling.

4. Cook the Stuffed Grape Leaves:

1. **Prepare Cooking Pot:** Place a few of the lemon slices in the bottom of a large pot. This helps prevent the grape leaves from sticking and adds flavor.
2. **Arrange Dolmas:** Place the stuffed grape leaves in the pot, seam side down. Arrange them tightly in layers if needed. Add the remaining lemon slices on top.
3. **Add Liquid:** Drizzle the olive oil over the top of the grape leaves and add 1 cup of water (or broth) to the pot.
4. **Simmer:** Cover the pot with a lid and bring to a gentle simmer over medium-low heat. Cook for 45-60 minutes, or until the grape leaves are tender and the filling is cooked through.

5. Serve:

1. **Cool Slightly:** Allow the dolmas to cool slightly before serving.
2. **Garnish:** Serve warm or at room temperature, garnished with additional fresh herbs or lemon wedges if desired.

Tips:

- **Leaf Preparation:** If the grape leaves are too tough, blanch them in boiling water for a few minutes to soften before using.
- **Flavor Variations:** Feel free to adjust the herbs and spices in the filling to your taste. You can also add currants or raisins for a touch of sweetness.

Enjoy your Stuffed Grape Leaves—a flavorful and versatile dish that's perfect as an appetizer, side, or main course!

Middle Eastern Spiced Chickpeas

Ingredients:

- **1 can (15 oz) chickpeas**, drained and rinsed (or 1 1/2 cups cooked chickpeas)
- **2 tablespoons olive oil**
- **1 teaspoon ground cumin**
- **1 teaspoon ground paprika** (or smoked paprika for extra depth)
- **1/2 teaspoon ground coriander**
- **1/2 teaspoon ground turmeric**
- **1/2 teaspoon ground cinnamon**
- **1/4 teaspoon ground cayenne pepper** (optional, for heat)
- **1/2 teaspoon garlic powder**
- **1/2 teaspoon onion powder**
- **Salt and freshly ground black pepper**, to taste
- **1 tablespoon fresh lemon juice** (or to taste)
- **Fresh parsley**, chopped, for garnish (optional)

Instructions:

1. Prepare the Chickpeas:

1. **Preheat Oven:** Preheat your oven to 400°F (200°C).
2. **Dry Chickpeas:** Pat the drained chickpeas dry with paper towels. Removing excess moisture helps them become crispy during roasting.

2. Season and Roast:

1. **Toss with Oil and Spices:** In a large bowl, combine the olive oil, ground cumin, paprika, coriander, turmeric, cinnamon, cayenne pepper (if using), garlic powder, onion powder, salt, and black pepper. Add the chickpeas and toss well to coat evenly.
2. **Roast Chickpeas:** Spread the seasoned chickpeas in a single layer on a baking sheet. Roast in the preheated oven for 25-30 minutes, or until the chickpeas are crispy and golden brown. Shake the pan or stir the chickpeas halfway through to ensure even cooking.

3. Finish and Serve:

1. **Add Lemon Juice:** Remove the chickpeas from the oven and let them cool slightly. Drizzle with fresh lemon juice and toss to coat.
2. **Garnish:** Garnish with chopped fresh parsley if desired.

4. Serve:

- **Enjoy Warm or Cold:** Serve the spiced chickpeas warm as a snack or side dish, or let them cool and use them as a crunchy topping for salads, grain bowls, or soups.

Tips:

- **For Extra Crispiness:** Make sure the chickpeas are thoroughly dried before roasting. You can also try roasting them a bit longer if you prefer them extra crispy.
- **Storage:** Store leftover spiced chickpeas in an airtight container at room temperature for up to 3 days. They can lose some crispness over time but can be refreshed in the oven for a few minutes.

Enjoy your Middle Eastern Spiced Chickpeas—a delicious and versatile snack or side dish packed with flavor and crunch!

Sumac Roasted Chicken

Ingredients:

- **1 whole chicken** (about 4-5 pounds), patted dry
- **2 tablespoons olive oil**
- **2 tablespoons ground sumac**
- **1 teaspoon ground cumin**
- **1 teaspoon ground paprika** (or smoked paprika)
- **1 teaspoon garlic powder**
- **1 teaspoon onion powder**
- **1 teaspoon dried oregano** (or dried thyme)
- **Salt and freshly ground black pepper**, to taste
- **1 lemon**, cut into wedges
- **4 cloves garlic**, minced
- **1 large onion**, quartered
- **Fresh herbs** (such as rosemary or thyme), for garnish (optional)

Instructions:

1. Prepare the Chicken:

1. **Preheat Oven:** Preheat your oven to 425°F (220°C).
2. **Season Chicken:** Rub the chicken all over with olive oil. In a small bowl, mix together the sumac, cumin, paprika, garlic powder, onion powder, oregano, salt, and black pepper. Rub this spice mixture evenly over the chicken, making sure to get some under the skin if possible.

2. Roast the Chicken:

1. **Stuff Chicken:** Place the minced garlic and onion quarters inside the cavity of the chicken. Squeeze a few lemon wedges over the chicken and place the squeezed lemon wedges inside the cavity as well.
2. **Roast Chicken:** Place the chicken breast-side up on a rack in a roasting pan. Roast in the preheated oven for 45-60 minutes, or until the chicken is golden brown and the internal temperature reaches 165°F (74°C) in the thickest part of the thigh. If the chicken starts to brown too quickly, you can cover it loosely with aluminum foil.

3. Finish and Serve:

1. **Rest Chicken:** Remove the chicken from the oven and let it rest for 10-15 minutes before carving. This allows the juices to redistribute and keeps the meat moist.
2. **Garnish:** Garnish with fresh herbs if desired and serve with additional lemon wedges on the side.

4. Serve:

- **Accompaniments:** Serve the Sumac Roasted Chicken with sides such as rice, couscous, roasted vegetables, or a fresh salad.

Tips:

- **Sumac:** Sumac adds a unique tartness that enhances the flavor of the chicken. If you can't find sumac, you can substitute with lemon zest or lemon juice, but the flavor will be different.
- **Crispy Skin:** For extra crispy skin, make sure the chicken is thoroughly dried before seasoning and roasting.
- **Vegetable Base:** You can add vegetables (like carrots, potatoes, or bell peppers) to the roasting pan. They will cook alongside the chicken and absorb some of the delicious flavors.

Enjoy your Sumac Roasted Chicken—a fragrant and tangy dish that brings a taste of the Middle East to your table!

Lentil Soup with Lemon

Ingredients:

- **2 tablespoons olive oil**
- **1 large onion**, diced
- **2 carrots**, diced
- **2 celery stalks**, diced
- **3 cloves garlic**, minced
- **1 teaspoon ground cumin**
- **1 teaspoon ground coriander**
- **1/2 teaspoon smoked paprika** (or regular paprika)
- **1/2 teaspoon dried thyme** (or 1 teaspoon fresh thyme)
- **1 1/2 cups dried green or brown lentils**, rinsed and drained
- **1 can (14.5 oz) diced tomatoes**, with juices
- **6 cups vegetable or chicken broth**
- **1 bay leaf**
- **Salt and freshly ground black pepper**, to taste
- **1 large lemon**, juiced (about 1/4 cup)
- **1 tablespoon lemon zest** (optional, for extra lemon flavor)
- **2 cups fresh spinach** or kale, chopped (optional, for added greens)
- **Chopped fresh parsley** (for garnish, optional)

Instructions:

1. Sauté Vegetables:

1. **Heat Oil:** In a large pot or Dutch oven, heat the olive oil over medium heat.
2. **Cook Vegetables:** Add the diced onion, carrots, and celery. Sauté for 5-7 minutes, or until the vegetables are softened and the onion is translucent.
3. **Add Garlic and Spices:** Stir in the minced garlic, ground cumin, ground coriander, paprika, and thyme. Cook for another 1-2 minutes, until fragrant.

2. Cook Lentils:

1. **Add Lentils and Tomatoes:** Add the rinsed lentils and diced tomatoes (with their juices) to the pot. Stir to combine.
2. **Add Broth and Bay Leaf:** Pour in the vegetable or chicken broth and add the bay leaf. Bring the mixture to a boil.
3. **Simmer:** Reduce the heat to low and let the soup simmer for 25-30 minutes, or until the lentils are tender.

3. Finish the Soup:

1. **Season:** Remove the bay leaf. Season the soup with salt and black pepper to taste.

2. **Add Lemon:** Stir in the lemon juice and lemon zest (if using). Adjust the seasoning as needed.
3. **Add Greens (Optional):** If using spinach or kale, stir it into the soup and cook for an additional 5 minutes, or until the greens are wilted and tender.

4. Serve:

1. **Garnish:** Ladle the soup into bowls and garnish with chopped fresh parsley if desired.
2. **Enjoy:** Serve the soup hot, with crusty bread or a side salad if you like.

Tips:

- **Lentils:** Green or brown lentils work best for this soup as they hold their shape well during cooking. Red lentils can also be used, but they will break down more and create a thicker soup.
- **Lemon Juice:** Adjust the amount of lemon juice to your taste preference. You can add more or less depending on how tangy you like your soup.
- **Storage:** Leftover soup can be stored in an airtight container in the refrigerator for up to 5 days. It also freezes well for up to 3 months.

Enjoy your Lentil Soup with Lemon—a nourishing and vibrant dish that's perfect for any time of the year!

Falafel with Tahini Sauce

Falafel Ingredients:

- **1 cup dried chickpeas** (not canned, soaked overnight in water)
- **1 small onion**, roughly chopped
- **3 cloves garlic**, minced
- **1/2 cup fresh parsley**, chopped
- **1/2 cup fresh cilantro**, chopped
- **1 teaspoon ground cumin**
- **1 teaspoon ground coriander**
- **1/2 teaspoon ground paprika**
- **1/4 teaspoon ground cayenne pepper** (optional, for heat)
- **1/2 teaspoon baking powder**
- **1/4 teaspoon baking soda** (optional, for extra fluffiness)
- **Salt and freshly ground black pepper**, to taste
- **1-2 tablespoons all-purpose flour** (if needed for binding)
- **Vegetable oil**, for frying

Tahini Sauce Ingredients:

- **1/2 cup tahini** (sesame paste)
- **1/4 cup fresh lemon juice** (about 1 lemon)
- **2-3 cloves garlic**, minced
- **1/4 cup water** (adjust as needed for consistency)
- **Salt**, to taste
- **1 tablespoon olive oil** (optional, for extra richness)

Instructions:

1. Prepare the Falafel:

1. **Soak Chickpeas:** Drain and rinse the soaked chickpeas. They should have doubled in size after soaking.
2. **Process Ingredients:** In a food processor, combine the chickpeas, chopped onion, garlic, parsley, and cilantro. Pulse until finely ground but still slightly coarse. Do not over-process into a paste.
3. **Add Spices:** Add the ground cumin, ground coriander, paprika, cayenne pepper (if using), baking powder, baking soda (if using), salt, and black pepper. Pulse to combine. If the mixture seems too wet or doesn't hold together, add 1-2 tablespoons of flour.
4. **Chill Mixture:** Transfer the mixture to a bowl, cover, and refrigerate for at least 30 minutes. This helps the mixture firm up and makes it easier to shape.

2. Shape and Fry Falafel:

1. **Shape Patties:** Using your hands or a falafel scoop, shape the mixture into small balls or patties, about 1-2 inches in diameter. Flatten them slightly for even cooking.
2. **Heat Oil:** Heat about 2-3 inches of vegetable oil in a deep skillet or pot to 350°F (175°C). You can test the oil by dropping a small piece of the mixture into it; it should sizzle and float to the top.
3. **Fry Falafel:** Fry the falafel in batches, being careful not to overcrowd the pan. Cook for 3-4 minutes, turning occasionally, until golden brown and crispy on all sides. Use a slotted spoon to transfer the falafel to a plate lined with paper towels to drain.

3. Prepare the Tahini Sauce:

1. **Mix Ingredients:** In a bowl, whisk together the tahini, lemon juice, minced garlic, and a pinch of salt. Gradually add water until you reach your desired consistency. The sauce should be creamy but pourable.
2. **Adjust Flavor:** Taste and adjust seasoning, adding more salt or lemon juice if needed. For extra richness, whisk in olive oil if desired.

4. Serve:

1. **Garnish:** Serve the falafel hot, drizzled with tahini sauce. You can also add toppings like sliced cucumbers, tomatoes, pickles, and fresh herbs.
2. **Accompaniments:** Enjoy with pita bread, or use in wraps or sandwiches. Pair with a side of tabbouleh, hummus, or a fresh salad for a complete meal.

Tips:

- **Consistency:** If the falafel mixture is too dry, add a bit of water. If it's too wet, add more flour.
- **Baking Option:** For a lighter version, you can bake the falafel at 375°F (190°C) for 25-30 minutes, flipping halfway through. They won't be as crispy as fried but are still delicious.
- **Freezing:** You can freeze uncooked falafel patties. Place them on a baking sheet to freeze individually, then transfer to a freezer bag. Fry or bake from frozen as needed.

Enjoy your homemade Falafel with Tahini Sauce—a delightful and satisfying dish that brings vibrant Middle Eastern flavors to your table!

Shawarma Beef Wraps

Ingredients:

For the Beef Marinade:

- 1 lb (450g) beef sirloin or flank steak, thinly sliced
- 3 tbsp olive oil
- 2 tbsp lemon juice
- 4 cloves garlic, minced
- 1 tbsp ground cumin
- 1 tbsp ground paprika
- 1 tbsp ground coriander
- 1 tbsp ground turmeric
- 1 tsp ground cinnamon
- 1 tsp ground allspice
- 1/2 tsp cayenne pepper (adjust to taste)
- Salt and black pepper to taste

For the Sauce:

- 1/2 cup plain Greek yogurt
- 2 tbsp tahini
- 1 tbsp lemon juice
- 1 clove garlic, minced
- Salt to taste

For the Wraps:

- Flatbreads or pita bread
- Sliced cucumbers
- Sliced tomatoes
- Shredded lettuce
- Pickled turnips or pickles
- Fresh parsley or cilantro, chopped (optional)

Instructions:

1. **Marinate the Beef:**
   - In a bowl, combine olive oil, lemon juice, minced garlic, cumin, paprika, coriander, turmeric, cinnamon, allspice, cayenne pepper, salt, and black pepper.
   - Add the sliced beef and toss to coat. Cover and refrigerate for at least 1 hour, or overnight for best results.
2. **Prepare the Sauce:**
   - In a bowl, mix together Greek yogurt, tahini, lemon juice, minced garlic, and a pinch of salt. Adjust seasoning to taste. Set aside.

3. **Cook the Beef:**
    - Heat a large skillet or grill pan over medium-high heat.
    - Add the marinated beef in batches (do not overcrowd the pan) and cook for about 3-4 minutes on each side, or until nicely browned and cooked through. Remove from heat and let rest for a few minutes.
4. **Assemble the Wraps:**
    - Warm the flatbreads or pita bread in a dry skillet or oven.
    - Spread a spoonful of the yogurt-tahini sauce on the bread.
    - Add a portion of the cooked beef.
    - Top with cucumbers, tomatoes, shredded lettuce, pickled turnips, and fresh parsley or cilantro if desired.
5. **Wrap and Serve:**
    - Fold the bread around the filling to form a wrap. You can also cut it in half if you prefer.
    - Serve immediately, or wrap in parchment paper for an on-the-go meal.

Enjoy your flavorful Shawarma beef wraps! They're perfect for a quick dinner or a tasty lunch.

Baba Ganoush

Ingredients:

- 2 medium eggplants
- 2 tbsp olive oil (plus more for drizzling)
- 1/4 cup tahini (sesame paste)
- 2 tbsp lemon juice (about 1 lemon)
- 2-3 cloves garlic, minced
- 1/2 tsp ground cumin
- 1/2 tsp smoked paprika (optional, for extra smokiness)
- Salt to taste
- Freshly ground black pepper to taste
- 2 tbsp chopped fresh parsley (optional, for garnish)
- Pomegranate seeds (optional, for garnish)

Instructions:

1. **Roast the Eggplants:**
   - Preheat your oven to 400°F (200°C). Alternatively, you can roast the eggplants over a gas burner for a more authentic smoky flavor.
   - Prick the eggplants with a fork several times to allow steam to escape.
   - Place the eggplants on a baking sheet and drizzle with olive oil.
   - Roast in the oven for about 35-40 minutes, turning occasionally, until the eggplants are soft and the skin is charred. If using a gas burner, roast the eggplants directly over the flame, turning occasionally, until the skin is charred and the flesh is soft.
   - Remove from the oven or burner and let them cool slightly.
2. **Prepare the Baba Ganoush:**
   - Once the eggplants are cool enough to handle, cut them in half and scoop out the flesh with a spoon, discarding the skin.
   - Place the eggplant flesh in a colander and let it drain for a few minutes to remove excess moisture.
   - Transfer the eggplant flesh to a food processor or blender.
3. **Blend the Ingredients:**
   - Add tahini, lemon juice, minced garlic, ground cumin, smoked paprika (if using), salt, and pepper to the food processor.
   - Blend until smooth and creamy. Taste and adjust seasoning if necessary.
4. **Serve:**
   - Transfer the Baba Ganoush to a serving bowl.
   - Drizzle with a little olive oil on top.
   - Garnish with chopped parsley and pomegranate seeds if desired.
   - Serve with pita bread, pita chips, or fresh vegetable sticks.

Baba Ganoush is perfect as an appetizer, a snack, or a side dish. Enjoy its rich, smoky flavor and creamy texture!

Roasted Eggplant Salad

Ingredients:

For the Salad:

- 2 medium eggplants, cut into 1-inch cubes
- 1 red bell pepper, chopped
- 1 yellow bell pepper, chopped
- 1 small red onion, diced
- 2-3 cloves garlic, minced
- 1-2 tbsp olive oil
- Salt and freshly ground black pepper to taste
- 1 cup cherry tomatoes, halved
- 1/2 cup Kalamata olives or green olives, pitted and sliced
- 1/4 cup fresh parsley, chopped
- 1/4 cup crumbled feta cheese (optional)

For the Dressing:

- 3 tbsp olive oil
- 2 tbsp balsamic vinegar (or red wine vinegar)
- 1 tsp Dijon mustard
- 1 clove garlic, minced
- 1/2 tsp dried oregano
- Salt and pepper to taste

Instructions:

1. **Roast the Vegetables:**
   - Preheat your oven to 425°F (220°C).
   - In a large bowl, toss the eggplant cubes, red and yellow bell peppers, diced onion, and minced garlic with olive oil, salt, and pepper.
   - Spread the vegetables in a single layer on a baking sheet.
   - Roast in the oven for 25-30 minutes, or until the eggplant is tender and the vegetables are nicely browned, stirring halfway through.
2. **Prepare the Dressing:**
   - In a small bowl or jar, whisk together the olive oil, balsamic vinegar, Dijon mustard, minced garlic, dried oregano, salt, and pepper until well combined.
3. **Assemble the Salad:**
   - In a large bowl, combine the roasted vegetables, cherry tomatoes, olives, and chopped parsley.
   - Drizzle with the dressing and toss to coat evenly.
   - Gently fold in the crumbled feta cheese, if using.
4. **Serve:**

- Serve the salad warm or at room temperature. It can also be chilled if you prefer.

This roasted eggplant salad is versatile and can be customized with additional ingredients like cucumbers, chickpeas, or avocado. Enjoy!

Moroccan Tagine with Apricots

Ingredients:

For the Tagine:

- **2 lbs (900g) lamb shoulder** or beef stew meat, cut into 1-inch cubes
- **2 tablespoons olive oil**
- **1 large onion**, chopped
- **3 cloves garlic**, minced
- **1 teaspoon ground cumin**
- **1 teaspoon ground coriander**
- **1 teaspoon ground cinnamon**
- **1/2 teaspoon ground ginger**
- **1/2 teaspoon turmeric**
- **1/2 teaspoon ground paprika**
- **1/4 teaspoon ground cayenne pepper** (optional, for heat)
- **1 cup dried apricots**, chopped
- **1 cup beef or vegetable broth**
- **1 can (14.5 oz) diced tomatoes**, with juices
- **1/2 cup almonds**, toasted and roughly chopped
- **1/2 cup green olives**, pitted and sliced (optional)
- **1/2 cup honey** (or to taste)
- **Salt and freshly ground black pepper**, to taste

For Garnish:

- **Fresh cilantro** or parsley, chopped
- **Toasted almonds** (optional)

Instructions:

1. Prepare the Tagine:

1. **Brown the Meat:** In a large tagine or Dutch oven, heat the olive oil over medium-high heat. Add the meat cubes and brown on all sides. You may need to do this in batches to avoid overcrowding the pan. Remove the browned meat and set aside.
2. **Sauté Vegetables:** In the same pot, add the chopped onion and cook until softened, about 5 minutes. Add the minced garlic and cook for another minute.
3. **Add Spices:** Stir in the cumin, coriander, cinnamon, ginger, turmeric, paprika, and cayenne pepper (if using). Cook for 1-2 minutes, until the spices are fragrant.
4. **Combine Ingredients:** Return the browned meat to the pot. Add the chopped dried apricots, broth, diced tomatoes (with their juices), and honey. Stir to combine.
5. **Simmer:** Bring the mixture to a boil, then reduce the heat to low. Cover and simmer for 1.5 to 2 hours, or until the meat is tender and cooked through. Stir occasionally and add more broth if needed to keep the meat covered.

2. Finish the Tagine:

1. **Add Almonds and Olives:** In the last 15 minutes of cooking, add the toasted almonds and green olives (if using). Adjust seasoning with salt and black pepper to taste.
2. **Adjust Sweetness:** Taste the tagine and adjust the sweetness by adding more honey if needed. The dish should have a balance of savory and sweet flavors.

3. Serve:

1. **Garnish:** Garnish the tagine with freshly chopped cilantro or parsley and additional toasted almonds if desired.
2. **Accompaniments:** Serve the tagine with couscous, rice, or warm flatbread to soak up the delicious sauce.

Tips:

- **Dried Apricots:** Soaking dried apricots in warm water for about 30 minutes before using them can make them plumper and juicier.
- **Cooking Equipment:** If you don't have a tagine, a Dutch oven or heavy-bottomed pot works well for this recipe.
- **Vegetarian Option:** For a vegetarian version, substitute the meat with chickpeas or a mix of vegetables like sweet potatoes and carrots.

Enjoy your Moroccan Tagine with Apricots—a delightful blend of sweet and savory flavors that brings a taste of Morocco to your table!

Stuffed Bell Peppers

Ingredients:

- **4 large bell peppers** (any color)
- **1 lb (450g) ground beef** or ground turkey (or a mix of meats)
- **1 small onion**, diced
- **2 cloves garlic**, minced
- **1 cup cooked rice** (white, brown, or a mix)
- **1 can (14.5 oz) diced tomatoes**, with juices
- **1/2 cup tomato sauce**
- **1 teaspoon dried oregano**
- **1 teaspoon dried basil**
- **1/2 teaspoon paprika**
- **1/2 teaspoon ground cumin**
- **Salt and freshly ground black pepper**, to taste
- **1 cup shredded cheese** (cheddar, mozzarella, or a blend), optional
- **2 tablespoons olive oil**

Instructions:

1. Prepare the Bell Peppers:

1. **Preheat Oven:** Preheat your oven to 375°F (190°C).
2. **Prepare Peppers:** Cut the tops off the bell peppers and remove the seeds and membranes. You can also trim a small slice off the bottom of the peppers to help them stand upright if needed.

2. Cook the Filling:

1. **Cook Meat:** In a large skillet, heat the olive oil over medium heat. Add the diced onion and cook until softened, about 5 minutes. Add the minced garlic and cook for another minute.
2. **Add Meat:** Add the ground beef or turkey to the skillet. Cook, breaking it up with a spoon, until fully browned and cooked through. Drain any excess fat.
3. **Combine Ingredients:** Stir in the cooked rice, diced tomatoes, tomato sauce, oregano, basil, paprika, cumin, salt, and black pepper. Cook for 5-7 minutes, allowing the flavors to meld and the mixture to thicken slightly.

3. Stuff the Peppers:

1. **Fill Peppers:** Spoon the meat and rice mixture into each bell pepper, packing it in firmly. Place the stuffed peppers upright in a baking dish.
2. **Add Cheese (Optional):** If using cheese, sprinkle it on top of each stuffed pepper.

4. Bake:

1. **Cover and Bake:** Cover the baking dish with aluminum foil and bake in the preheated oven for 30 minutes.
2. **Uncover and Finish:** Remove the foil and bake for an additional 10-15 minutes, or until the peppers are tender and the cheese is melted and bubbly (if using).

5. Serve:

1. **Garnish:** Let the stuffed peppers cool for a few minutes before serving. Garnish with fresh herbs like parsley or basil if desired.

Tips:

- **Variation:** You can add other ingredients to the filling, such as black beans, corn, or chopped vegetables for extra flavor and nutrition.
- **Rice:** If you prefer, you can use quinoa or couscous instead of rice.
- **Freezing:** Stuffed peppers can be frozen before baking. Assemble and freeze them in a single layer on a baking sheet, then transfer to a freezer bag. Bake from frozen, adding extra time as needed.

Enjoy your Stuffed Bell Peppers—a comforting, flavorful dish that's easy to customize and perfect for a hearty meal!

Hummus with Pine Nuts

Ingredients:

- **1 can (15 oz) chickpeas**, drained and rinsed (or 1.5 cups cooked chickpeas)
- **1/4 cup tahini** (sesame paste)
- **1/4 cup fresh lemon juice** (about 1 lemon)
- **2-3 cloves garlic**, minced
- **1/4 cup extra-virgin olive oil**, plus more for drizzling
- **1/2 teaspoon ground cumin**
- **Salt and freshly ground black pepper**, to taste
- **2-3 tablespoons water** (adjust as needed for consistency)
- **1/4 cup pine nuts**, toasted
- **Paprika or sumac**, for garnish (optional)
- **Fresh parsley**, chopped, for garnish (optional)

Instructions:

1. Prepare the Hummus:

1. **Blend Ingredients:** In a food processor, combine the chickpeas, tahini, lemon juice, and minced garlic. Process until smooth, scraping down the sides as needed.
2. **Add Olive Oil and Spices:** With the processor running, slowly add the olive oil and blend until fully incorporated. Add the ground cumin, salt, and black pepper. Blend again until smooth.
3. **Adjust Consistency:** If the hummus is too thick, add water a tablespoon at a time until you reach your desired consistency. The hummus should be creamy and spreadable.

2. Toast the Pine Nuts:

1. **Toast Pine Nuts:** In a small, dry skillet over medium heat, toast the pine nuts, stirring frequently, until golden and fragrant. This usually takes about 2-3 minutes. Be careful not to burn them.

3. Assemble and Serve:

1. **Transfer Hummus:** Spoon the hummus into a serving bowl. Use the back of a spoon to create a small well in the center.
2. **Top with Pine Nuts:** Sprinkle the toasted pine nuts over the hummus.
3. **Drizzle and Garnish:** Drizzle a little extra-virgin olive oil over the top. Optionally, sprinkle with paprika or sumac and garnish with fresh parsley.
4. **Serve:** Serve with pita bread, pita chips, fresh vegetables, or as part of a larger mezze platter.

Tips:

- **Tahini:** For the best flavor, use good-quality tahini. If it's too thick, you can thin it out with a little water before adding to the hummus.
- **Garlic:** Adjust the amount of garlic to your taste. Raw garlic can be quite strong, so start with less if you prefer a milder flavor.
- **Consistency:** Hummus can be made ahead of time and stored in an airtight container in the refrigerator for up to a week. It may thicken slightly, so stir in a bit more water or olive oil before serving if needed.

Enjoy your Hummus with Pine Nuts—a delicious and nutritious dip that's perfect for any occasion!

Grilled Kofta

Ingredients:

- **1 lb (450g) ground beef** (or a mix of beef and lamb)
- **1 small onion**, finely grated
- **2 cloves garlic**, minced
- **1/4 cup fresh parsley**, finely chopped
- **1/4 cup fresh cilantro**, finely chopped
- **1 teaspoon ground cumin**
- **1 teaspoon ground coriander**
- **1/2 teaspoon ground paprika**
- **1/2 teaspoon ground cinnamon**
- **1/4 teaspoon ground allspice**
- **1/4 teaspoon ground black pepper**
- **1/2 teaspoon salt**
- **1/4 teaspoon cayenne pepper** (optional, for heat)
- **1 tablespoon olive oil** (for mixing)
- **Wooden skewers**, soaked in water (if using)

Instructions:

1. Prepare the Kofta Mixture:

1. **Combine Ingredients:** In a large bowl, combine the ground meat, grated onion, minced garlic, parsley, cilantro, cumin, coriander, paprika, cinnamon, allspice, black pepper, salt, and cayenne pepper (if using). Add the olive oil and mix everything together until well combined. It's best to use your hands to ensure the spices and herbs are evenly distributed throughout the meat.
2. **Chill Mixture:** Cover the bowl and refrigerate the mixture for at least 30 minutes. This helps the flavors meld together and makes it easier to shape the kofta.

2. Shape and Skewer:

1. **Shape Kofta:** Take small portions of the meat mixture and mold them around skewers, forming elongated shapes. Press the meat firmly onto the skewers to help it hold its shape while grilling.
2. **Preheat Grill:** Preheat your grill to medium-high heat. If using a charcoal grill, let the coals burn until they are covered with a thin layer of ash.

3. Grill the Kofta:

1. **Grill Kofta:** Place the skewers on the grill and cook for about 8-10 minutes, turning occasionally, until the kofta is browned and cooked through. The internal temperature should reach 160°F (71°C).
2. **Rest:** Remove the kofta from the grill and let it rest for a few minutes before serving.

4. Serve:

1. **Garnish:** Serve the grilled kofta with your favorite accompaniments, such as pita bread, hummus, tzatziki, or a fresh salad. Garnish with additional chopped parsley or cilantro if desired.
2. **Accompaniments:** Kofta pairs well with rice or couscous, and can be enjoyed with roasted vegetables or a yogurt-based sauce.

Tips:

- **Meat Choice:** For a more traditional flavor, use a mix of ground beef and lamb. If you prefer a leaner option, you can use only ground beef.
- **Spices:** Adjust the spices to suit your taste. For extra depth of flavor, try adding a pinch of smoked paprika or a dash of ground nutmeg.
- **Soaking Skewers:** If using wooden skewers, soak them in water for at least 30 minutes before grilling to prevent them from burning.

Enjoy your Grilled Kofta—a flavorful and satisfying dish that's perfect for outdoor gatherings or a delicious meal at home!

Saffron Rice with Raisins

Ingredients:

- **1 1/2 cups basmati rice**
- **2 tablespoons olive oil** or **butter**
- **1 small onion**, finely chopped
- **1/4 cup raisins**
- **1/4 teaspoon saffron threads**
- **1/4 cup warm water** (for saffron)
- **2 cups water** or **chicken broth**
- **1 teaspoon salt**
- **1/2 teaspoon ground cumin** (optional)
- **1/4 teaspoon ground cinnamon** (optional)
- **1/4 cup slivered almonds** or **pine nuts**, toasted (for garnish, optional)
- **Fresh parsley** or **cilantro**, chopped (for garnish, optional)

Instructions:

1. Prepare the Saffron:

1. **Soak Saffron:** Place the saffron threads in a small bowl and add the warm water. Let it soak for about 10 minutes to release its color and flavor.

2. Cook the Rice:

1. **Rinse Rice:** Rinse the basmati rice under cold water until the water runs clear. This removes excess starch and helps the rice stay fluffy.
2. **Cook Onion:** In a medium saucepan, heat the olive oil or butter over medium heat. Add the chopped onion and cook until softened and lightly golden, about 5 minutes.
3. **Add Raisins:** Stir in the raisins and cook for another 1-2 minutes.
4. **Combine Rice and Spices:** Add the rinsed rice to the saucepan and stir to coat with the onion and raisins. If using, add the ground cumin and ground cinnamon at this point.
5. **Add Liquid:** Pour in the 2 cups of water or chicken broth and add the salt. Stir to combine. Bring the mixture to a boil.
6. **Simmer:** Once boiling, reduce the heat to low, cover, and simmer for 15-20 minutes, or until the rice is tender and the liquid is absorbed.

3. Incorporate Saffron:

1. **Add Saffron:** Gently fluff the rice with a fork. Pour the saffron water over the rice and stir gently to distribute the saffron evenly throughout the rice.

4. Garnish and Serve:

1. **Garnish:** If desired, top the rice with toasted slivered almonds or pine nuts and chopped fresh parsley or cilantro.
2. **Serve:** Serve the saffron rice warm as a side dish with your favorite main courses, such as grilled meats, stews, or roasted vegetables.

Tips:

- **Saffron Quality:** Use high-quality saffron for the best flavor and color. A little goes a long way, so use sparingly.
- **Toasting Nuts:** To toast almonds or pine nuts, place them in a dry skillet over medium heat, stirring frequently until golden and fragrant. This usually takes 2-3 minutes.
- **Rice Texture:** Avoid stirring the rice too much during cooking to prevent it from becoming mushy.

Enjoy your Saffron Rice with Raisins—a delightful and aromatic dish that adds a touch of elegance to any meal!

Harissa-Spiced Carrots

Ingredients:

- **1 lb (450g) carrots**, peeled and cut into sticks or rounds
- **2 tablespoons olive oil**
- **2 tablespoons harissa paste** (adjust to taste)
- **1 teaspoon ground cumin**
- **1/2 teaspoon smoked paprika**
- **1/2 teaspoon ground coriander**
- **Salt and freshly ground black pepper**, to taste
- **1 tablespoon honey** or **maple syrup** (optional, for added sweetness)
- **Fresh cilantro** or **parsley**, chopped, for garnish (optional)
- **Lemon wedges**, for serving (optional)

Instructions:

1. Preheat Oven:

1. **Preheat Oven:** Preheat your oven to 425°F (220°C).

2. Prepare Carrots:

1. **Prepare Carrots:** Peel and cut the carrots into sticks or rounds. Try to keep them evenly sized for uniform cooking.

3. Season Carrots:

1. **Mix Spices:** In a large bowl, combine the olive oil, harissa paste, ground cumin, smoked paprika, ground coriander, salt, and black pepper. Mix well.
2. **Coat Carrots:** Add the carrot pieces to the bowl and toss to coat them evenly with the harissa mixture.

4. Roast Carrots:

1. **Roast:** Spread the coated carrots in a single layer on a baking sheet. Roast in the preheated oven for 20-25 minutes, or until the carrots are tender and slightly caramelized. Stir once halfway through cooking for even roasting.
2. **Optional Sweetener:** If you prefer a touch of sweetness, drizzle the honey or maple syrup over the carrots in the last 5 minutes of roasting.

5. Serve:

1. **Garnish:** Remove the carrots from the oven and transfer them to a serving dish. Garnish with fresh chopped cilantro or parsley if desired.

2. **Accompaniments:** Serve with lemon wedges on the side for a fresh squeeze of lemon juice, which adds a nice balance to the spicy harissa.

Tips:

- **Harissa Paste:** Adjust the amount of harissa paste based on your heat preference. Start with less if you're sensitive to spice and add more to taste.
- **Roasting Pan:** Use parchment paper or a silicone baking mat on your baking sheet for easier cleanup and to prevent sticking.
- **Storage:** Leftovers can be stored in an airtight container in the refrigerator for up to 3-4 days. Reheat in the oven to retain the texture.

Enjoy your Harissa-Spiced Carrots—a vibrant and spicy side dish that pairs well with a variety of main courses!

Chicken with Olives and Preserved Lemons

Ingredients:

- **1 whole chicken** (about 3-4 lbs), cut into pieces
- **2 tablespoons olive oil**
- **1 large onion**, finely chopped
- **3 cloves garlic**, minced
- **1 teaspoon ground ginger**
- **1 teaspoon ground cumin**
- **1 teaspoon ground coriander**
- **1/2 teaspoon ground turmeric**
- **1/2 teaspoon paprika**
- **1/4 teaspoon ground cinnamon**
- **1/4 teaspoon cayenne pepper** (optional, for heat)
- **1/2 cup green olives**, pitted and sliced
- **1/2 cup preserved lemons**, rinsed and cut into strips (about 2 lemons)
- **1 cup chicken broth**
- **1 tablespoon honey** or **maple syrup** (optional, for sweetness)
- **Fresh cilantro** or **parsley**, chopped, for garnish (optional)

Instructions:

1. Prepare the Chicken:

1. **Season Chicken:** Pat the chicken pieces dry with paper towels. Season with salt and pepper on both sides.

2. Sear the Chicken:

1. **Heat Oil:** In a large, heavy-bottomed pot or Dutch oven, heat the olive oil over medium-high heat.
2. **Sear Chicken:** Add the chicken pieces, skin-side down, and cook until browned, about 5-7 minutes per side. You may need to do this in batches. Remove the chicken and set aside.

3. Prepare the Sauce:

1. **Cook Onion:** In the same pot, add the chopped onion and cook until softened and golden, about 5 minutes.
2. **Add Garlic and Spices:** Add the minced garlic, ground ginger, cumin, coriander, turmeric, paprika, cinnamon, and cayenne pepper (if using). Cook for another minute until the spices are fragrant.
3. **Deglaze and Simmer:** Pour in the chicken broth and scrape up any browned bits from the bottom of the pot. Stir to combine.

4. Cook the Chicken:

1. **Add Chicken:** Return the chicken pieces to the pot, along with any juices that have collected. Bring the mixture to a boil.
2. **Simmer:** Reduce the heat to low, cover, and simmer for 30-40 minutes, or until the chicken is cooked through and tender.

5. Add Olives and Preserved Lemons:

1. **Add Olives and Lemons:** Stir in the sliced olives and preserved lemon strips. Simmer for an additional 10-15 minutes, allowing the flavors to meld together.
2. **Optional Sweetener:** If desired, add honey or maple syrup for a touch of sweetness. Stir well.

6. Serve:

1. **Garnish:** Garnish with chopped fresh cilantro or parsley if desired.
2. **Accompaniments:** Serve the chicken with couscous, rice, or crusty bread to soak up the flavorful sauce.

Tips:

- **Preserved Lemons:** If you can't find preserved lemons, you can use fresh lemon slices, though the flavor will be slightly different. Make sure to adjust the quantity of lemon juice or zest to taste.
- **Olives:** Use good-quality green olives for the best flavor. You can also use black olives if you prefer.
- **Cooking Time:** If using bone-in, skin-on chicken pieces, the cooking time may be longer. Ensure the chicken reaches an internal temperature of 165°F (74°C).

Enjoy your Chicken with Olives and Preserved Lemons—a savory and tangy dish that brings a touch of Moroccan cuisine to your table!

Tabbouleh Salad

Ingredients:

- **1 cup fine bulgur wheat**
- **1 1/2 cups boiling water**
- **1 large bunch of fresh parsley** (about 2 cups, finely chopped)
- **1/2 cup fresh mint leaves** (finely chopped)
- **2 medium tomatoes**, diced
- **1 cucumber**, peeled and diced
- **1 small red onion**, finely chopped
- **1/4 cup extra-virgin olive oil**
- **1/4 cup fresh lemon juice** (about 2 lemons)
- **Salt**, to taste
- **Freshly ground black pepper**, to taste

Instructions:

1. Prepare the Bulgur:

1. **Soak Bulgur:** Place the bulgur in a large bowl and pour the boiling water over it. Stir to combine, then cover the bowl with a clean kitchen towel or plastic wrap. Let it sit for about 20-30 minutes, or until the bulgur is tender and the water is absorbed. Fluff with a fork to separate the grains.

2. Prepare the Vegetables and Herbs:

1. **Chop Herbs:** While the bulgur is soaking, finely chop the parsley and mint. You want to chop them as finely as possible for the best texture.
2. **Dice Vegetables:** Dice the tomatoes and cucumber, and finely chop the red onion.

3. Combine Salad Ingredients:

1. **Mix Ingredients:** In a large bowl, combine the cooked bulgur, chopped parsley, mint, tomatoes, cucumber, and red onion.

4. Dress the Salad:

1. **Prepare Dressing:** In a small bowl or jar, whisk together the olive oil, lemon juice, salt, and black pepper.
2. **Toss Salad:** Pour the dressing over the salad and toss well to coat all the ingredients evenly.

5. Chill and Serve:

1. **Chill:** Let the tabbouleh salad chill in the refrigerator for at least 30 minutes before serving. This allows the flavors to meld together.
2. **Serve:** Serve cold or at room temperature as a refreshing side dish or light main course.

Tips:

- **Bulgur Wheat:** Make sure to use fine bulgur for the traditional texture of tabbouleh. Coarse bulgur can be used but will result in a different texture.
- **Herbs:** Use fresh parsley and mint for the best flavor. Dried herbs will not provide the same freshness.
- **Lemon Juice:** Adjust the amount of lemon juice to your taste. Some people prefer a tangier salad, while others may like it milder.

Enjoy your Tabbouleh Salad—a vibrant, flavorful dish that's perfect for any meal or gathering!

Mujadara (Lentil and Rice Pilaf)

Ingredients:

- **1 cup green or brown lentils**
- **1/2 cup basmati rice**
- **4 cups water or vegetable broth**
- **2 large onions**, thinly sliced
- **1/4 cup olive oil**
- **1 teaspoon ground cumin**
- **1/2 teaspoon ground coriander**
- **1/2 teaspoon ground cinnamon**
- **1/4 teaspoon ground allspice**
- **Salt and freshly ground black pepper**, to taste
- **Chopped fresh parsley** (for garnish, optional)
- **Plain yogurt** or **Tzatziki** (for serving, optional)

Instructions:

1. Cook the Lentils:

1. **Rinse Lentils:** Rinse the lentils under cold water and remove any debris.
2. **Cook Lentils:** In a medium pot, add the lentils and 2 cups of water or vegetable broth. Bring to a boil, then reduce the heat to low and simmer for about 15-20 minutes, or until the lentils are tender but not mushy. Drain and set aside.

2. Prepare the Rice:

1. **Rinse Rice:** Rinse the basmati rice under cold water until the water runs clear.
2. **Cook Rice:** In a separate pot, add the rice and 1 1/2 cups of water or vegetable broth. Bring to a boil, then reduce the heat to low, cover, and simmer for about 15 minutes, or until the rice is tender and the liquid is absorbed. Remove from heat and let it sit, covered, for 5 minutes. Fluff with a fork and set aside.

3. Caramelize the Onions:

1. **Heat Oil:** In a large skillet, heat the olive oil over medium heat.
2. **Cook Onions:** Add the sliced onions and cook, stirring occasionally, until they become golden brown and caramelized, about 15-20 minutes. Be patient and stir often to ensure even caramelization. Remove from heat.

4. Combine Lentils and Rice:

1. **Mix Ingredients:** In a large bowl, combine the cooked lentils and rice.
2. **Add Spices:** Stir in the ground cumin, coriander, cinnamon, allspice, salt, and black pepper. Adjust the seasoning to taste.

5. Serve:

1. **Top with Onions:** Transfer the lentil and rice mixture to a serving dish and top with the caramelized onions.
2. **Garnish:** Garnish with chopped fresh parsley if desired.
3. **Accompaniments:** Serve the Mujadara with plain yogurt or tzatziki on the side, and optionally with a fresh salad or pickles.

Tips:

- **Caramelizing Onions:** Caramelizing onions can take some time, but it's worth the effort for the deep, sweet flavor they add to the dish.
- **Lentils:** Green or brown lentils work best for this recipe. Red lentils tend to become mushy and are not ideal for this dish.
- **Rice:** For extra flavor, you can cook the rice with a small amount of the onion oil used for caramelizing or add a bit of garlic.

Enjoy your Mujadara—a hearty, comforting dish that's perfect for a satisfying meal!

Fattoush Salad

Ingredients:

- **2 large pita breads** (or 4 small), cut into triangles
- **2 tablespoons olive oil**
- **1 teaspoon ground sumac** (optional, but adds authentic flavor)
- **4 cups mixed salad greens** (such as romaine, arugula, or spinach), chopped
- **1 large cucumber**, diced
- **2 medium tomatoes**, diced
- **1 bell pepper**, diced (any color)
- **1 small red onion**, thinly sliced
- **1/2 cup radishes**, thinly sliced
- **1/4 cup fresh parsley**, chopped
- **1/4 cup fresh mint leaves**, chopped
- **1/4 cup fresh basil** (optional), chopped
- **1/4 cup fresh lemon juice** (about 2 lemons)
- **1/4 cup extra-virgin olive oil**
- **1 tablespoon pomegranate molasses** (optional, for a tangy sweetness)
- **Salt and freshly ground black pepper**, to taste

Instructions:

1. Prepare the Pita Bread:

1. **Preheat Oven:** Preheat your oven to 400°F (200°C).
2. **Season Pita:** Brush the pita bread triangles with olive oil and sprinkle with a bit of salt and ground sumac if using.
3. **Bake:** Arrange the pita triangles in a single layer on a baking sheet. Bake for about 5-7 minutes, or until they are crispy and golden brown. Remove from the oven and let cool.

2. Prepare the Vegetables and Herbs:

1. **Chop Vegetables:** Dice the cucumber, tomatoes, and bell pepper. Thinly slice the red onion and radishes.
2. **Chop Herbs:** Finely chop the parsley, mint, and basil if using.

3. Prepare the Dressing:

1. **Mix Dressing:** In a small bowl or jar, whisk together the lemon juice, olive oil, pomegranate molasses (if using), salt, and black pepper.

4. Assemble the Salad:

1. **Combine Ingredients:** In a large salad bowl, combine the chopped salad greens, cucumber, tomatoes, bell pepper, red onion, radishes, parsley, mint, and basil.

2. **Add Dressing:** Pour the dressing over the salad and toss well to combine.
3. **Add Pita:** Gently fold in the crispy pita bread pieces just before serving to keep them crunchy.

5. Serve:

1. **Serve Immediately:** Fattoush is best enjoyed immediately after adding the pita to maintain its crispiness.

Tips:

- **Sumac:** Sumac adds a tangy flavor to the salad, but if you can't find it, you can skip it or use a small amount of lemon zest as a substitute.
- **Pita:** Make sure the pita is completely crisp before adding it to the salad to avoid sogginess.
- **Fresh Herbs:** Fresh herbs are key to the salad's flavor, so don't skip them if possible. Adjust the amount based on your preference.

Enjoy your Fattoush Salad—a colorful, flavorful dish that's perfect for a light meal or as a side for various main courses!

Yogurt-Marinated Chicken

Ingredients:

- **4 boneless, skinless chicken breasts** or **thighs**
- **1 cup plain Greek yogurt** (or regular yogurt)
- **2 tablespoons olive oil**
- **2 tablespoons lemon juice** (about 1 lemon)
- **3 cloves garlic**, minced
- **1 teaspoon ground cumin**
- **1 teaspoon ground paprika** (sweet or smoked)
- **1 teaspoon ground coriander**
- **1/2 teaspoon ground turmeric**
- **1/2 teaspoon ground cinnamon**
- **1/4 teaspoon ground black pepper**
- **1 teaspoon salt** (or to taste)
- Fresh **cilantro** or **parsley** for garnish (optional)

Instructions:

1. Prepare the Marinade:

1. **Mix Ingredients:** In a large bowl, combine the Greek yogurt, olive oil, lemon juice, minced garlic, ground cumin, paprika, coriander, turmeric, cinnamon, black pepper, and salt. Mix well until all the ingredients are thoroughly combined.

2. Marinate the Chicken:

1. **Coat Chicken:** Add the chicken pieces to the bowl with the marinade. Toss to coat the chicken evenly with the marinade.
2. **Marinate:** Cover the bowl with plastic wrap or transfer the chicken and marinade to a resealable plastic bag. Refrigerate for at least 1 hour, or up to 8 hours for best results. If marinating for longer, you may want to stir occasionally to ensure even marination.

3. Cook the Chicken:

1. **Preheat Oven or Grill:** If cooking in the oven, preheat to 400°F (200°C). If grilling, preheat your grill to medium-high heat.
2. **Cook Chicken:**
   - **Oven:** Place the marinated chicken on a baking sheet lined with parchment paper or a lightly greased rack. Bake for 25-30 minutes, or until the chicken is cooked through and reaches an internal temperature of 165°F (74°C).
   - **Grill:** Place the marinated chicken on the grill and cook for 5-7 minutes per side, or until the chicken is cooked through and has nice grill marks.

4. Serve:

1. **Rest Chicken:** Let the chicken rest for a few minutes after cooking to retain its juices.
2. **Garnish:** Garnish with chopped fresh cilantro or parsley if desired.
3. **Serve:** Serve the yogurt-marinated chicken with your favorite side dishes, such as rice, couscous, or a fresh salad.

Tips:

- **Marinade:** The yogurt marinade helps to tenderize the chicken, making it juicy and flavorful. Don't skip the marination step for the best results.
- **Cooking Method:** You can also cook the marinated chicken in a skillet over medium heat. Just be sure to cook it through completely.
- **Leftovers:** Store any leftovers in an airtight container in the refrigerator for up to 3-4 days.

Enjoy your Yogurt-Marinated Chicken—a delicious and succulent dish with a wonderful blend of spices and tangy yogurt flavor!

Moroccan Chickpea Stew

Ingredients:

- **2 tablespoons olive oil**
- **1 large onion**, chopped
- **3 cloves garlic**, minced
- **1 large carrot**, peeled and diced
- **1 bell pepper**, diced (any color)
- **1 medium zucchini**, diced
- **1 can (14.5 oz) diced tomatoes**, with juices
- **1 can (15 oz) chickpeas**, drained and rinsed
- **1 cup vegetable broth** (or chicken broth)
- **1 teaspoon ground cumin**
- **1 teaspoon ground coriander**
- **1 teaspoon ground paprika** (sweet or smoked)
- **1/2 teaspoon ground turmeric**
- **1/2 teaspoon ground cinnamon**
- **1/4 teaspoon ground allspice**
- **1/4 teaspoon ground cayenne pepper** (optional, for heat)
- **Salt and freshly ground black pepper**, to taste
- **1/2 cup raisins** or **dried apricots**, chopped (optional, for sweetness)
- **1/2 cup chopped fresh cilantro** or **parsley**, for garnish
- **Lemon wedges**, for serving (optional)

Instructions:

1. Sauté Vegetables:

1. **Heat Oil:** In a large pot or Dutch oven, heat the olive oil over medium heat.
2. **Cook Onions:** Add the chopped onion and cook until softened and translucent, about 5 minutes.
3. **Add Garlic:** Add the minced garlic and cook for another minute, until fragrant.

2. Add Spices and Vegetables:

1. **Add Spices:** Stir in the ground cumin, coriander, paprika, turmeric, cinnamon, allspice, and cayenne pepper if using. Cook for about 1 minute to toast the spices.
2. **Add Vegetables:** Add the diced carrot, bell pepper, and zucchini. Cook for 5-7 minutes, stirring occasionally, until the vegetables start to soften.

3. Add Liquids and Simmer:

1. **Add Tomatoes and Chickpeas:** Stir in the diced tomatoes with their juices and the chickpeas.
2. **Add Broth:** Pour in the vegetable broth and bring the mixture to a boil.

3. **Simmer:** Reduce the heat to low, cover, and simmer for 20-25 minutes, or until the vegetables are tender.
4. **Optional Sweetener:** If using, stir in the raisins or chopped dried apricots. Simmer for an additional 5 minutes.

4. Season and Serve:

1. **Season:** Taste and adjust seasoning with salt and black pepper as needed.
2. **Garnish:** Garnish with chopped fresh cilantro or parsley.
3. **Serve:** Serve the stew hot with lemon wedges on the side, and optionally with couscous, rice, or crusty bread.

Tips:

- **Spices:** Adjust the spices to your taste. Moroccan cuisine is known for its complex spice blends, so feel free to experiment with the amounts.
- **Sweetness:** The raisins or dried apricots add a nice sweetness that balances the savory spices. If you prefer a less sweet stew, you can omit them.
- **Vegetables:** You can add other vegetables to the stew, such as sweet potatoes, butternut squash, or green beans, depending on what you have on hand.

Enjoy your Moroccan Chickpea Stew—a rich, comforting dish that brings the flavors of Morocco right to your table!

Date and Nut Couscous

Ingredients:

- **1 cup couscous**
- **1 cup vegetable or chicken broth** (or water)
- **2 tablespoons olive oil** or **butter**
- **1/2 cup dates**, pitted and chopped
- **1/2 cup nuts**, such as almonds, walnuts, or pecans, chopped
- **1/4 cup fresh parsley**, chopped
- **1/4 cup fresh mint**, chopped (optional)
- **1/4 teaspoon ground cinnamon**
- **1/4 teaspoon ground cumin** (optional)
- **Salt and freshly ground black pepper**, to taste
- **1 tablespoon lemon juice** (optional, for added brightness)

Instructions:

1. Prepare the Couscous:

1. **Boil Liquid:** In a medium saucepan, bring the vegetable or chicken broth (or water) to a boil.
2. **Add Couscous:** Stir in the couscous, cover the pot, and remove it from the heat. Let it sit for 5 minutes to allow the couscous to absorb the liquid.
3. **Fluff Couscous:** After 5 minutes, remove the lid and fluff the couscous with a fork.

2. Prepare the Add-ins:

1. **Toast Nuts:** In a small skillet, heat the olive oil or butter over medium heat. Add the chopped nuts and cook, stirring frequently, until they are golden brown and fragrant, about 3-5 minutes. Remove from heat and set aside.
2. **Chop Dates:** While the nuts are toasting, chop the dates into small pieces.

3. Combine Ingredients:

1. **Mix Ingredients:** In a large bowl, combine the fluffed couscous with the chopped dates, toasted nuts, ground cinnamon, and ground cumin (if using). Stir well to combine.
2. **Add Fresh Herbs:** Gently fold in the chopped fresh parsley and mint, if using.
3. **Season:** Season with salt and black pepper to taste. Add lemon juice if desired for extra brightness.

4. Serve:

1. **Serve Warm:** Serve the Date and Nut Couscous warm as a side dish or light main course. It pairs well with grilled meats, stews, or as part of a larger spread.

Tips:

- **Nuts:** You can use any nuts you prefer or have on hand. Toasting them enhances their flavor and crunch.
- **Dates:** For a richer flavor, you can use Medjool dates, which are larger and sweeter. Adjust the amount of dates based on your preference for sweetness.
- **Herbs:** Fresh herbs add a burst of flavor and color. If you don't have mint, parsley alone works fine.

Enjoy your Date and Nut Couscous—a sweet and savory dish with a delightful texture and flavor profile!

Roasted Cauliflower with Cumin

Ingredients:

- **1 large head of cauliflower**, cut into florets
- **2 tablespoons olive oil**
- **1 teaspoon ground cumin**
- **1/2 teaspoon ground paprika** (optional, for extra flavor)
- **1/2 teaspoon garlic powder** (optional)
- **Salt**, to taste
- **Freshly ground black pepper**, to taste
- **Fresh lemon juice** (optional, for finishing)
- **Chopped fresh cilantro** or **parsley** (for garnish, optional)

Instructions:

1. Preheat Oven:

1. **Preheat Oven:** Preheat your oven to 425°F (220°C).

2. Prepare Cauliflower:

1. **Cut Cauliflower:** Remove the leaves from the cauliflower and cut it into bite-sized florets.
2. **Season:** In a large bowl, toss the cauliflower florets with olive oil, ground cumin, paprika, garlic powder (if using), salt, and black pepper. Make sure the cauliflower is evenly coated with the seasoning.

3. Roast the Cauliflower:

1. **Arrange on Baking Sheet:** Spread the seasoned cauliflower florets in a single layer on a baking sheet. Make sure they're not crowded to ensure even roasting.
2. **Roast:** Roast in the preheated oven for 25-30 minutes, or until the cauliflower is golden brown and tender, with some crispy edges. Toss halfway through the cooking time for even roasting.

4. Finish and Serve:

1. **Add Lemon Juice (Optional):** For added brightness, drizzle the roasted cauliflower with fresh lemon juice just before serving.
2. **Garnish (Optional):** Garnish with chopped fresh cilantro or parsley if desired.
3. **Serve:** Serve the roasted cauliflower warm as a side dish or part of a larger meal.

Tips:

- **Cauliflower Size:** Cut the cauliflower into evenly sized pieces to ensure they cook evenly.
- **Cumin:** Ground cumin adds a warm, earthy flavor, but you can also experiment with other spices like coriander or turmeric if you like.
- **Crispiness:** For extra crispiness, you can broil the cauliflower for an additional 1-2 minutes at the end of cooking. Watch it closely to avoid burning.

Enjoy your Roasted Cauliflower with Cumin—an easy, flavorful dish that pairs well with a variety of main courses and adds a delicious touch to your meal!

Chicken Shawarma Salad

Ingredients:

For the Chicken Marinade:

- 1 lb (450 g) boneless, skinless chicken thighs
- 3 tbsp olive oil
- 2 tbsp lemon juice
- 4 cloves garlic, minced
- 1 tbsp ground cumin
- 1 tbsp ground paprika
- 1 tbsp ground turmeric
- 1 tsp ground coriander
- 1 tsp ground allspice
- 1 tsp ground cinnamon
- 1 tsp cayenne pepper (optional, for heat)
- Salt and black pepper to taste

For the Salad:

- 6 cups mixed greens (e.g., lettuce, spinach, arugula)
- 1 cucumber, sliced
- 1 cup cherry tomatoes, halved
- 1 red onion, thinly sliced
- 1/2 cup kalamata olives, pitted
- 1/2 cup crumbled feta cheese (optional)
- 1/4 cup fresh parsley, chopped

For the Dressing:

- 1/4 cup tahini
- 3 tbsp lemon juice
- 2 tbsp olive oil
- 2 tbsp water (to thin out the dressing)
- 1 clove garlic, minced
- Salt and black pepper to taste

Instructions:

1. **Marinate the Chicken:**
   - In a large bowl, mix together the olive oil, lemon juice, garlic, cumin, paprika, turmeric, coriander, allspice, cinnamon, cayenne pepper, salt, and black pepper.
   - Add the chicken thighs to the marinade and toss to coat. Cover and refrigerate for at least 1 hour, or up to overnight for better flavor.

2. **Cook the Chicken:**
    - Preheat your grill or skillet over medium-high heat.
    - Cook the chicken thighs for 5-7 minutes per side, or until fully cooked and the internal temperature reaches 165°F (74°C). Allow to rest for a few minutes, then slice into strips.
3. **Prepare the Salad:**
    - In a large bowl, combine the mixed greens, cucumber, cherry tomatoes, red onion, olives, feta cheese, and parsley.
4. **Make the Dressing:**
    - In a small bowl, whisk together the tahini, lemon juice, olive oil, water, garlic, salt, and black pepper until smooth. Adjust seasoning and consistency as needed.
5. **Assemble the Salad:**
    - Top the salad with the sliced chicken. Drizzle with the tahini dressing or serve it on the side.
6. **Serve:**
    - Toss the salad if desired, and serve immediately. Enjoy!

Feel free to customize the salad with additional toppings or ingredients based on your preferences!

Moussaka

Ingredients:

For the Meat Sauce:

- 2 tbsp olive oil
- 1 large onion, finely chopped
- 3 cloves garlic, minced
- 1 lb (450 g) ground beef or lamb
- 1 (14.5 oz/400 g) can diced tomatoes
- 2 tbsp tomato paste
- 1/2 cup red wine (optional)
- 1 tsp ground cinnamon
- 1 tsp dried oregano
- 1/2 tsp ground allspice
- Salt and black pepper to taste

For the Eggplant:

- 2-3 large eggplants, sliced into 1/4-inch rounds
- Olive oil for brushing
- Salt

For the Béchamel Sauce:

- 4 tbsp butter
- 1/4 cup all-purpose flour
- 2 cups whole milk
- 1/2 cup grated Parmesan cheese (or kefalotyri cheese if available)
- 1/4 tsp ground nutmeg
- 2 large eggs, beaten
- Salt and black pepper to taste

Additional Ingredients:

- 1/2 cup grated Parmesan cheese (for topping)

Instructions:

1. **Prepare the Eggplant:**
   - Preheat your oven to 400°F (200°C).
   - Arrange the eggplant slices in a single layer on baking sheets. Brush both sides with olive oil and sprinkle with salt.

- Bake for about 20 minutes, turning halfway through, until the eggplants are tender and lightly browned. Set aside.

2. **Make the Meat Sauce:**
    - Heat olive oil in a large skillet over medium heat. Add the onion and cook until translucent.
    - Add garlic and cook for another minute.
    - Add the ground beef or lamb and cook until browned. Drain excess fat if necessary.
    - Stir in diced tomatoes, tomato paste, red wine (if using), cinnamon, oregano, allspice, salt, and pepper.
    - Simmer for about 20-30 minutes, until the sauce has thickened. Adjust seasoning to taste.

3. **Prepare the Béchamel Sauce:**
    - In a medium saucepan, melt the butter over medium heat.
    - Add flour and cook, stirring constantly, for about 1-2 minutes.
    - Gradually whisk in the milk and cook until the sauce thickens and is smooth.
    - Stir in the grated Parmesan cheese, nutmeg, salt, and pepper.
    - Remove from heat and allow to cool slightly, then whisk in the beaten eggs.

4. **Assemble the Moussaka:**
    - Preheat your oven to 350°F (175°C).
    - In a large baking dish, spread a layer of eggplant slices on the bottom.
    - Spread half of the meat sauce over the eggplant.
    - Add another layer of eggplant, followed by the remaining meat sauce.
    - Pour the béchamel sauce over the top, spreading it evenly. Sprinkle with additional grated Parmesan cheese.

5. **Bake:**
    - Bake in the preheated oven for about 45-60 minutes, or until the top is golden brown and the moussaka is bubbly.
    - Let the moussaka cool for about 15-20 minutes before serving to allow the layers to set.

6. **Serve:**
    - Cut into squares and serve warm. Enjoy your delicious homemade moussaka!

Feel free to adapt the recipe by adding other vegetables or using different types of meat if desired.

Spiced Couscous with Dried Fruit

Ingredients:

- 1 cup couscous
- 1 cup chicken or vegetable broth (or water)
- 2 tbsp olive oil or butter
- 1 small onion, finely chopped
- 2 cloves garlic, minced
- 1/2 tsp ground cumin
- 1/2 tsp ground coriander
- 1/2 tsp ground cinnamon
- 1/4 tsp ground turmeric
- 1/4 tsp ground paprika
- 1/4 tsp ground black pepper
- Salt to taste
- 1/2 cup dried apricots, chopped
- 1/2 cup dried cranberries or raisins
- 1/4 cup almonds or pine nuts, toasted (optional)
- 1/4 cup fresh parsley or cilantro, chopped (for garnish)
- 1-2 tbsp honey or maple syrup (optional, for added sweetness)

Instructions:

1. **Prepare the Couscous:**
    - In a medium saucepan, bring the broth (or water) to a boil.
    - Stir in the couscous, cover, and remove from heat. Let it sit for 5 minutes, then fluff with a fork.
2. **Cook the Aromatics:**
    - While the couscous is resting, heat the olive oil or butter in a large skillet over medium heat.
    - Add the chopped onion and cook until softened, about 3-4 minutes.
    - Stir in the garlic and cook for an additional 1 minute.
3. **Add Spices:**
    - Add the cumin, coriander, cinnamon, turmeric, paprika, black pepper, and salt to the skillet. Stir well to coat the onions and garlic with the spices.
4. **Combine with Couscous:**
    - Add the cooked couscous to the skillet, mixing it with the spiced onion and garlic mixture.
    - Stir in the dried apricots and dried cranberries (or raisins).
    - If using, add the toasted almonds or pine nuts.
5. **Add Sweetener (Optional):**
    - If you prefer a slightly sweeter dish, drizzle in honey or maple syrup and mix well.
6. **Garnish and Serve:**

- Garnish with chopped fresh parsley or cilantro before serving.

This spiced couscous pairs well with a variety of dishes, from roasted meats to grilled vegetables. Enjoy!

Eggplant and Tomato Stew

Ingredients:

- 2 large eggplants, diced into 1-inch cubes
- 2 tbsp olive oil
- 1 large onion, chopped
- 3 cloves garlic, minced
- 1 red bell pepper, chopped
- 1 green bell pepper, chopped
- 1 (14.5 oz/400 g) can diced tomatoes
- 1 cup tomato sauce
- 1/2 cup vegetable or chicken broth
- 1 tsp ground cumin
- 1 tsp dried oregano
- 1/2 tsp ground paprika
- 1/2 tsp ground cinnamon (optional)
- 1/4 tsp red pepper flakes (optional, for heat)
- Salt and black pepper to taste
- 1/4 cup fresh basil or parsley, chopped (for garnish)
- 1 tbsp lemon juice (optional, for a bit of brightness)

Instructions:

1. **Prepare the Eggplant:**
    - Place the diced eggplant in a colander, sprinkle with salt, and let it sit for about 30 minutes to draw out excess moisture and bitterness. Rinse and pat dry with paper towels.
2. **Cook the Eggplant:**
    - Heat the olive oil in a large skillet or Dutch oven over medium heat.
    - Add the eggplant cubes and cook until golden and tender, about 8-10 minutes. Remove the eggplant from the skillet and set aside.
3. **Cook the Vegetables:**
    - In the same skillet, add a bit more olive oil if needed. Add the chopped onion and cook until translucent, about 5 minutes.
    - Stir in the garlic and cook for another minute until fragrant.
    - Add the chopped bell peppers and cook for about 5 minutes until they start to soften.
4. **Add Tomatoes and Spices:**
    - Stir in the diced tomatoes, tomato sauce, and broth.
    - Add the ground cumin, dried oregano, paprika, cinnamon (if using), red pepper flakes (if using), salt, and black pepper. Mix well.
5. **Simmer the Stew:**
    - Return the cooked eggplant to the skillet and stir to combine.

- Bring the mixture to a boil, then reduce heat and let it simmer uncovered for about 20-25 minutes, or until the vegetables are tender and the flavors are well combined. Adjust seasoning as needed.
6. **Finish and Serve:**
    - If using, stir in the lemon juice to brighten the flavors.
    - Garnish with chopped fresh basil or parsley before serving.

This stew is delicious on its own or served over rice, couscous, or with a side of crusty bread. It also makes a great accompaniment to grilled meats or a hearty addition to a vegetarian meal. Enjoy!

Lamb and Spinach Stew

Ingredients:

- 1.5 lbs (700 g) lamb shoulder or stew meat, cut into 1-inch cubes
- 2 tbsp olive oil
- 1 large onion, chopped
- 3 cloves garlic, minced
- 2 carrots, sliced
- 2 celery stalks, chopped
- 1 red bell pepper, chopped
- 1 (14.5 oz/400 g) can diced tomatoes
- 1 cup beef or vegetable broth
- 1 cup dry white wine (optional, or use additional broth)
- 1 tsp ground cumin
- 1 tsp ground coriander
- 1/2 tsp ground cinnamon
- 1/2 tsp paprika
- 1/4 tsp ground turmeric (optional)
- 1/4 tsp red pepper flakes (optional, for heat)
- Salt and black pepper to taste
- 4 cups fresh spinach, washed and trimmed
- 1/4 cup fresh parsley or cilantro, chopped (for garnish)
- 1 tbsp lemon juice (optional, for brightness)

Instructions:

1. **Brown the Lamb:**
   - Heat the olive oil in a large pot or Dutch oven over medium-high heat.
   - Add the lamb cubes in batches, being careful not to overcrowd the pot. Brown the lamb on all sides, then remove and set aside. Repeat with remaining lamb if necessary.
2. **Cook the Aromatics:**
   - In the same pot, add the chopped onion and cook until softened, about 5 minutes.
   - Stir in the garlic and cook for an additional minute until fragrant.
3. **Add Vegetables and Spices:**
   - Add the carrots, celery, and red bell pepper. Cook for about 5 minutes, stirring occasionally.
   - Stir in the ground cumin, ground coriander, cinnamon, paprika, turmeric (if using), red pepper flakes (if using), salt, and black pepper.
4. **Deglaze and Simmer:**
   - Return the browned lamb to the pot. Add the diced tomatoes, beef or vegetable broth, and white wine (or additional broth).

- Bring the mixture to a boil, then reduce the heat to low and cover. Simmer for 1.5 to 2 hours, or until the lamb is tender and the flavors have melded together.
5. **Add Spinach:**
    - Stir in the fresh spinach a handful at a time, allowing it to wilt before adding more. Continue until all the spinach is incorporated and wilted, about 5 minutes.
6. **Finish and Serve:**
    - If using, stir in the lemon juice to brighten the flavors.
    - Garnish with chopped fresh parsley or cilantro before serving.

Serve the lamb and spinach stew hot, with a side of rice, couscous, or crusty bread to soak up the flavorful broth. Enjoy your hearty and satisfying meal!

Greek Lemon Potatoes

Ingredients:

- 2 lbs (900 g) baby potatoes or small Yukon Gold potatoes
- 1/4 cup olive oil
- 1/4 cup fresh lemon juice (about 2 lemons)
- 1/4 cup chicken or vegetable broth
- 4 cloves garlic, minced
- 1 tbsp dried oregano
- 1 tsp dried thyme (optional)
- 1 tsp ground paprika
- 1/2 tsp ground black pepper
- 1 tsp salt (or to taste)
- 1/4 cup fresh parsley, chopped (for garnish)
- Lemon wedges (for serving)

Instructions:

1. **Prepare the Potatoes:**
   - Preheat your oven to 400°F (200°C).
   - Wash and scrub the potatoes. If they are large, cut them into wedges; if they are baby potatoes, you can leave them whole or halve them.
2. **Make the Lemon Mixture:**
   - In a bowl, whisk together the olive oil, lemon juice, chicken or vegetable broth, minced garlic, dried oregano, dried thyme (if using), paprika, black pepper, and salt.
3. **Season the Potatoes:**
   - Place the potatoes in a large baking dish or roasting pan.
   - Pour the lemon mixture over the potatoes and toss to coat them evenly.
4. **Roast the Potatoes:**
   - Spread the potatoes out in a single layer in the baking dish.
   - Roast in the preheated oven for about 45-60 minutes, turning the potatoes halfway through, until they are golden brown and crispy on the edges, and tender when pierced with a fork.
5. **Finish and Serve:**
   - Garnish with chopped fresh parsley.
   - Serve with lemon wedges on the side for an extra burst of freshness.

These Greek lemon potatoes are aromatic and flavorful, with a perfect balance of tangy lemon and savory spices. They're a great addition to any meal and pair especially well with Greek-style grilled meats, fish, or even a simple salad. Enjoy!

Za'atar Roasted Chicken

Ingredients:

- 1 whole chicken (about 4-5 lbs/1.8-2.3 kg)
- 3 tbsp olive oil
- 3 tbsp za'atar spice blend
- 1 lemon, cut into wedges
- 4 cloves garlic, minced
- Salt and black pepper to taste
- Fresh parsley or cilantro, chopped (for garnish)

For the Za'atar Spice Blend (if not using a pre-made blend):

- 2 tbsp dried thyme
- 1 tbsp sesame seeds
- 1 tbsp ground sumac
- 1/2 tsp salt

Instructions:

1. **Prepare the Spice Blend:**
    - If you're making your own za'atar spice blend, mix the dried thyme, sesame seeds, ground sumac, and salt in a small bowl. Set aside.
2. **Prepare the Chicken:**
    - Preheat your oven to 425°F (220°C).
    - Pat the chicken dry with paper towels to ensure a crispy skin.
    - Rub the chicken all over with olive oil.
3. **Season the Chicken:**
    - Rub the za'atar spice blend evenly over the entire surface of the chicken.
    - Season the chicken generously with salt and black pepper.
    - Place the minced garlic inside the cavity of the chicken.
4. **Roast the Chicken:**
    - Place the chicken in a roasting pan or on a baking sheet. Squeeze the lemon wedges over the chicken and place them inside the cavity along with any remaining garlic.
    - Roast the chicken in the preheated oven for about 1 to 1.5 hours, or until the skin is golden brown and crispy, and the internal temperature reaches 165°F (74°C) when checked with a meat thermometer in the thickest part of the thigh.
5. **Rest and Serve:**
    - Remove the chicken from the oven and let it rest for about 10-15 minutes before carving.
    - Garnish with chopped fresh parsley or cilantro.

Serve the za'atar roasted chicken with your favorite sides, such as roasted vegetables, rice, or a fresh salad. The za'atar gives the chicken a unique and aromatic flavor that's sure to impress!

Caramelized Onion Rice

Ingredients:

- 1 cup long-grain white rice (or your preferred variety)
- 2 cups chicken or vegetable broth
- 2 large onions, thinly sliced
- 2 tbsp olive oil or butter
- 1 tbsp brown sugar (optional, for extra caramelization)
- 2 cloves garlic, minced
- 1 tsp dried thyme or rosemary (optional)
- Salt and black pepper to taste
- Fresh parsley or chives, chopped (for garnish)

Instructions:

1. **Cook the Rice:**
    - Rinse the rice under cold water until the water runs clear.
    - In a medium saucepan, bring the chicken or vegetable broth to a boil.
    - Add the rice, reduce the heat to low, cover, and simmer for 15-20 minutes, or until the rice is cooked and the liquid is absorbed. Remove from heat and let it sit, covered, for 5 minutes. Fluff with a fork.
2. **Caramelize the Onions:**
    - While the rice is cooking, heat the olive oil or butter in a large skillet over medium heat.
    - Add the sliced onions and cook, stirring occasionally, for about 15-20 minutes, or until the onions are deeply browned and caramelized. If using, stir in the brown sugar about halfway through the cooking time to enhance the caramelization.
    - Stir in the minced garlic and cook for an additional 1-2 minutes until fragrant.
3. **Combine and Season:**
    - Once the onions are caramelized, stir in the cooked rice. Mix well to combine and let the flavors meld together for a few minutes.
    - Add dried thyme or rosemary if using, and season with salt and black pepper to taste.
4. **Serve:**
    - Garnish with chopped fresh parsley or chives before serving.

This caramelized onion rice pairs beautifully with roasted meats, grilled vegetables, or as a stand-alone dish. Enjoy the rich, sweet flavor of the caramelized onions combined with the savory rice!

Persian Chicken Kebabs

Ingredients:

For the Marinade:

- 1 cup plain Greek yogurt
- 1/4 cup fresh lemon juice (about 2 lemons)
- 1/4 cup olive oil
- 4 cloves garlic, minced
- 1 tbsp ground cumin
- 1 tbsp ground coriander
- 1/2 tsp ground turmeric
- 1/2 tsp ground paprika
- 1/4 tsp ground cinnamon (optional)
- 1/2 tsp saffron threads, soaked in 2 tbsp hot water (optional, for color and flavor)
- Salt and black pepper to taste

For the Kebabs:

- 2 lbs (900 g) boneless, skinless chicken thighs, cut into 1-inch cubes
- 1 large onion, cut into wedges
- 1 bell pepper, cut into chunks (optional)
- 1-2 tomatoes, cut into wedges (optional)
- Fresh parsley or cilantro, chopped (for garnish)

For Serving (optional):

- Pita bread or flatbreads
- Hummus or tzatziki
- Grilled vegetables or rice (such as Persian saffron rice)

Instructions:

1. **Prepare the Marinade:**
    - In a large bowl, mix together the Greek yogurt, lemon juice, olive oil, minced garlic, ground cumin, ground coriander, turmeric, paprika, cinnamon (if using), saffron water (if using), salt, and black pepper.
2. **Marinate the Chicken:**
    - Add the chicken cubes to the marinade and toss to coat evenly. Cover and refrigerate for at least 2 hours, or up to overnight for best results.
3. **Prepare the Skewers:**
    - If using wooden skewers, soak them in water for at least 30 minutes to prevent burning. If using metal skewers, they don't need pre-soaking.

- Thread the marinated chicken onto the skewers, alternating with onion wedges, bell pepper chunks, and tomato wedges if using.
4. **Grill the Kebabs:**
    - Preheat your grill to medium-high heat. You can also use a grill pan or broiler if a grill isn't available.
    - Place the skewers on the grill and cook for about 10-15 minutes, turning occasionally, until the chicken is cooked through and has nice grill marks. The internal temperature should reach 165°F (74°C).
5. **Serve:**
    - Remove the kebabs from the grill and let them rest for a few minutes.
    - Garnish with chopped fresh parsley or cilantro.
    - Serve with pita bread or flatbreads, hummus or tzatziki, and grilled vegetables or rice if desired.

These Persian chicken kebabs are flavorful, juicy, and perfect for a summer barbecue or a delicious meal any time of the year. Enjoy!

Lebanese Meat Pies

Ingredients:

For the Dough:

- 2 1/4 tsp (1 packet) active dry yeast
- 1 cup warm water (about 110°F/45°C)
- 1 tbsp sugar
- 3 1/2 cups all-purpose flour
- 1/4 cup olive oil
- 1 tsp salt

For the Filling:

- 1 lb (450 g) ground beef or lamb
- 1 large onion, finely chopped
- 2 cloves garlic, minced
- 1/2 cup pine nuts or almonds (optional), toasted
- 1 tomato, finely chopped
- 1/4 cup fresh parsley or cilantro, chopped
- 1 tsp ground cumin
- 1/2 tsp ground allspice
- 1/2 tsp ground cinnamon
- 1/4 tsp ground black pepper
- Salt to taste
- 2 tbsp olive oil

For Garnish (optional):

- 1/4 cup pomegranate seeds
- Lemon wedges

Instructions:

1. **Prepare the Dough:**
    - In a small bowl, dissolve the sugar in warm water and then sprinkle the yeast over the top. Let it sit for about 5-10 minutes, until it becomes frothy.
    - In a large bowl, mix the flour and salt. Create a well in the center and pour in the yeast mixture and olive oil. Stir until a dough forms.
    - Knead the dough on a floured surface for about 5-7 minutes, until it's smooth and elastic.
    - Place the dough in a lightly oiled bowl, cover with a damp cloth or plastic wrap, and let it rise in a warm place for about 1 hour, or until doubled in size.
2. **Prepare the Filling:**

- Heat olive oil in a large skillet over medium heat. Add the chopped onion and cook until softened, about 5 minutes.
- Add the minced garlic and cook for an additional minute.
- Add the ground beef or lamb, and cook until browned. Drain excess fat if needed.
- Stir in the finely chopped tomato, pine nuts (if using), parsley or cilantro, cumin, allspice, cinnamon, black pepper, and salt. Cook for another 5 minutes, until the mixture is well combined and the flavors meld together. Remove from heat and let cool.

3. **Assemble the Pies:**
   - Preheat your oven to 375°F (190°C).
   - Punch down the risen dough and divide it into 12-16 equal pieces.
   - Roll each piece into a small circle (about 4-5 inches in diameter) on a floured surface.
   - Place a spoonful of the meat filling in the center of each circle.
   - Fold up the sides to form a triangular or half-moon shape, pinching the edges to seal. You can also fold in the sides to create an open-faced pie.
   - Place the assembled pies on a baking sheet lined with parchment paper.

4. **Bake the Pies:**
   - Bake in the preheated oven for about 15-20 minutes, or until the pies are golden brown.

5. **Garnish and Serve:**
   - If desired, garnish with pomegranate seeds and serve with lemon wedges on the side.

These Lebanese meat pies are delicious warm or at room temperature. They make a great addition to any meal or can be enjoyed as a tasty snack. Enjoy!

Sautéed Spinach with Garlic

Ingredients:

- 2 tbsp olive oil
- 3-4 cloves garlic, thinly sliced or minced
- 10-12 oz (280-340 g) fresh spinach (about 10 cups of raw spinach)
- Salt and black pepper to taste
- 1/4 tsp red pepper flakes (optional, for a bit of heat)
- 1 tbsp lemon juice (optional, for added brightness)

Instructions:

1. **Prepare the Spinach:**
   - Wash the spinach thoroughly and pat dry with paper towels or use a salad spinner to remove excess water. If the spinach leaves are large, you can roughly chop them.
2. **Sauté the Garlic:**
   - Heat the olive oil in a large skillet over medium heat.
   - Add the sliced or minced garlic and cook for about 1-2 minutes, stirring frequently, until the garlic is fragrant and lightly golden. Be careful not to let it burn.
3. **Cook the Spinach:**
   - Add the spinach to the skillet, a handful at a time if necessary. Stir constantly to ensure even cooking.
   - Cook the spinach for about 2-3 minutes, or until wilted. The spinach will reduce significantly in volume as it cooks.
4. **Season and Finish:**
   - Season with salt, black pepper, and red pepper flakes (if using). Stir well to combine.
   - If desired, add the lemon juice for a touch of brightness and stir to incorporate.
5. **Serve:**
   - Transfer the sautéed spinach to a serving dish and serve immediately.

This simple and flavorful sautéed spinach with garlic is a great way to enjoy a healthy green vegetable with minimal fuss. It pairs well with everything from grilled meats to pasta dishes, or can be enjoyed on its own as a light side.

Fennel and Orange Salad

Ingredients:

- 2 large fennel bulbs
- 2 large oranges
- 1/4 red onion, thinly sliced (optional)
- 1/4 cup Kalamata olives, pitted and sliced (optional)
- 1/4 cup fresh parsley or mint, chopped
- 2 tbsp extra-virgin olive oil
- 1 tbsp red wine vinegar or lemon juice
- Salt and black pepper to taste
- 1/4 tsp fennel seeds (optional, for extra flavor)

Instructions:

1. **Prepare the Fennel:**
   - Trim the fennel bulbs by cutting off the stalks and fronds. Save some fronds for garnish if desired.
   - Slice the fennel bulbs thinly using a mandoline or a sharp knife. For a more delicate texture, you can also shave the fennel.
2. **Prepare the Oranges:**
   - Peel the oranges, removing the white pith, and segment them by cutting between the membranes. You can also cut them into bite-sized pieces if preferred.
   - Collect any juice that escapes while segmenting the oranges and set aside.
3. **Assemble the Salad:**
   - In a large bowl, combine the sliced fennel, orange segments, and thinly sliced red onion (if using).
   - Add the Kalamata olives and chopped parsley or mint.
4. **Make the Dressing:**
   - In a small bowl, whisk together the olive oil, red wine vinegar or lemon juice, and any reserved orange juice. Season with salt and black pepper to taste.
   - Add the fennel seeds if using.
5. **Toss the Salad:**
   - Pour the dressing over the fennel and orange mixture.
   - Gently toss to combine, making sure everything is evenly coated with the dressing.
6. **Garnish and Serve:**
   - Garnish with reserved fennel fronds if desired.
   - Serve immediately or let it sit for about 15 minutes to allow the flavors to meld together.

This fennel and orange salad is light, refreshing, and full of bright flavors. It pairs wonderfully with seafood, grilled meats, or can be enjoyed on its own for a light meal. Enjoy!

Moroccan Carrot Salad

Ingredients:

- 1 lb (450 g) carrots, peeled and cut into thin rounds or julienned
- 2 tbsp olive oil
- 2 tbsp fresh lemon juice
- 1 tsp ground cumin
- 1/2 tsp ground coriander
- 1/2 tsp ground paprika
- 1/2 tsp ground cinnamon
- 1/4 tsp ground turmeric (optional)
- 1/4 tsp ground cayenne pepper (optional, for heat)
- 2 tbsp chopped fresh parsley or cilantro
- 2 tbsp toasted almonds or pine nuts (optional)
- Salt and black pepper to taste

Instructions:

1. **Cook the Carrots:**
   - Bring a large pot of salted water to a boil.
   - Add the carrots and cook until tender but still crisp, about 4-5 minutes. Be careful not to overcook them.
   - Drain the carrots and immediately transfer them to a bowl of ice water to stop the cooking process and preserve their bright color. Drain again after a few minutes and pat dry with paper towels.
2. **Prepare the Dressing:**
   - In a large bowl, whisk together the olive oil, lemon juice, ground cumin, ground coriander, paprika, cinnamon, turmeric (if using), cayenne pepper (if using), salt, and black pepper.
3. **Combine Ingredients:**
   - Add the cooked carrots to the bowl with the dressing. Toss to coat the carrots evenly with the spices and dressing.
4. **Add Herbs and Nuts:**
   - Stir in the chopped parsley or cilantro.
   - If using, sprinkle the toasted almonds or pine nuts on top for added crunch and flavor.
5. **Serve:**
   - The salad can be served immediately or allowed to marinate in the refrigerator for at least 30 minutes to enhance the flavors.
   - Taste and adjust seasoning if necessary before serving.

This Moroccan carrot salad is colorful and full of flavor, making it a wonderful addition to any meal. It pairs well with grilled meats, couscous, or can be enjoyed on its own as a light and refreshing dish.

Almond and Honey Baklava

Ingredients:

For the Baklava:

- 1 package (16 oz/450 g) phyllo dough, thawed
- 1 1/2 cups almonds, finely chopped
- 1 cup unsalted butter, melted
- 1 tsp ground cinnamon

For the Honey Syrup:

- 1 cup honey
- 1 cup granulated sugar
- 1 cup water
- 1 tsp lemon juice
- 1 cinnamon stick (optional)
- 1 strip of lemon peel (optional)

Instructions:

1. **Prepare the Nuts:**
   - In a bowl, combine the finely chopped almonds and ground cinnamon. Set aside.
2. **Prepare the Phyllo Dough:**
   - Preheat your oven to 350°F (175°C).
   - Unroll the phyllo dough and cover it with a damp kitchen towel to prevent it from drying out.
3. **Assemble the Baklava:**
   - Brush a 9x13-inch baking dish with melted butter.
   - Place one sheet of phyllo dough in the dish and brush it with melted butter. Repeat this process, layering and buttering each sheet, until you have about 8 sheets layered.
   - Sprinkle a thin layer of the almond mixture evenly over the top.
   - Continue layering and buttering phyllo sheets, adding a layer of almonds every 4-5 sheets, until you use up the nuts and phyllo dough. Finish with about 8-10 more layers of phyllo dough, each brushed with butter.
4. **Cut the Baklava:**
   - Use a sharp knife to cut the baklava into diamond or square shapes, making sure to cut all the way through to the bottom of the dish.
5. **Bake:**
   - Bake in the preheated oven for 45-55 minutes, or until the baklava is golden brown and crisp.
6. **Prepare the Syrup:**

- While the baklava is baking, prepare the syrup. In a saucepan, combine the honey, granulated sugar, and water.
- Bring to a boil over medium heat, stirring occasionally until the sugar is dissolved.
- Add the lemon juice, cinnamon stick, and lemon peel if using. Reduce heat and simmer for about 10 minutes. Remove from heat and let cool.

7. **Finish the Baklava:**
    - When the baklava comes out of the oven, immediately pour the cooled syrup evenly over the hot baklava. Allow it to cool completely and absorb the syrup, about 2-3 hours.

8. **Serve:**
    - Once cooled, the baklava can be cut into pieces along the pre-cut lines. Serve and enjoy!

This almond and honey baklava is a sweet and crunchy treat that's sure to impress. It pairs wonderfully with a cup of tea or coffee. Enjoy your homemade baklava!

Yogurt-Cucumber Dip

Ingredients:

- 1 cup plain Greek yogurt (or regular plain yogurt, strained)
- 1 medium cucumber
- 2 cloves garlic, minced
- 2 tbsp fresh dill, chopped (or mint, if preferred)
- 1 tbsp extra-virgin olive oil
- 1 tbsp fresh lemon juice
- Salt and black pepper to taste

Instructions:

1. **Prepare the Cucumber:**
   - Peel the cucumber if desired, and cut it in half lengthwise. Use a spoon to scoop out the seeds.
   - Grate the cucumber using a box grater or food processor. If you prefer a smoother texture, you can chop it finely instead of grating.
   - Place the grated cucumber in a clean kitchen towel or cheesecloth and squeeze out as much excess moisture as possible. This step is important to prevent the dip from becoming watery.
2. **Mix the Dip:**
   - In a medium bowl, combine the Greek yogurt, minced garlic, chopped dill (or mint), olive oil, and lemon juice.
   - Stir in the prepared cucumber and mix well.
3. **Season and Chill:**
   - Season the dip with salt and black pepper to taste. Adjust the seasoning if necessary.
   - Cover and refrigerate for at least 30 minutes to allow the flavors to meld. The dip can be made a day ahead for even better flavor.
4. **Serve:**
   - Serve chilled with pita bread, fresh vegetables, or as a side with grilled meats.

This yogurt-cucumber dip is creamy, tangy, and packed with fresh flavors. It's perfect for summer gatherings, as a cooling side dish, or a healthy snack. Enjoy!

Rosewater Rice Pudding

Ingredients:

- 1/2 cup short-grain or Arborio rice
- 2 cups whole milk
- 1/2 cup heavy cream
- 1/2 cup granulated sugar
- 1/4 tsp salt
- 1/4 cup water
- 1/4 tsp rosewater (adjust to taste, as it's quite strong)
- 1/4 tsp ground cardamom (optional, for extra flavor)
- 1 tbsp cornstarch (optional, for a thicker consistency)
- Fresh rose petals (optional, for garnish)

Instructions:

1. **Cook the Rice:**
   - Rinse the rice under cold water until the water runs clear.
   - In a medium saucepan, combine the rice and water. Cook over medium heat until the water is mostly absorbed and the rice is tender, about 10 minutes.
2. **Prepare the Pudding:**
   - In a separate saucepan, combine the milk, heavy cream, sugar, and salt. Heat over medium heat until the mixture is hot but not boiling.
   - Add the cooked rice to the milk mixture and cook over low heat, stirring frequently, for about 20-25 minutes, or until the pudding thickens and the rice is very soft.
3. **Thicken the Pudding (Optional):**
   - If you prefer a thicker pudding, mix the cornstarch with 2 tablespoons of cold milk to form a slurry. Stir this slurry into the pudding and cook for an additional 5 minutes until thickened.
4. **Add Flavor:**
   - Remove the saucepan from heat and stir in the rosewater and ground cardamom (if using). Taste and adjust the amount of rosewater if needed.
5. **Cool and Serve:**
   - Transfer the rice pudding to serving bowls or dishes. Allow it to cool to room temperature, then refrigerate for at least 2 hours to chill and set.
6. **Garnish:**
   - Before serving, garnish with fresh rose petals if desired.

This rosewater rice pudding is a delightful dessert with a subtle floral aroma and creamy texture. It's perfect for special occasions or as a soothing treat anytime. Enjoy!

Stuffed Acorn Squash

Ingredients:

For the Acorn Squash:

- 2 acorn squash
- 2 tbsp olive oil
- Salt and black pepper to taste

For the Stuffing:

- 1 cup quinoa, farro, or rice (cooked according to package instructions)
- 1 tbsp olive oil
- 1 onion, finely chopped
- 2 cloves garlic, minced
- 1 cup mushrooms, diced (optional)
- 1 cup spinach or kale, chopped
- 1/2 cup dried cranberries or raisins
- 1/4 cup nuts (e.g., walnuts, pecans, or almonds), chopped and toasted
- 1/2 cup feta cheese or shredded cheese of your choice (optional)
- 1 tsp dried thyme or rosemary (or 1 tbsp fresh)
- 1/2 tsp ground cumin (optional)
- Salt and black pepper to taste

Instructions:

1. **Prepare the Acorn Squash:**
   - Preheat your oven to 400°F (200°C).
   - Cut the acorn squash in half lengthwise and scoop out the seeds.
   - Brush the cut sides with olive oil and season with salt and black pepper.
   - Place the squash halves cut-side down on a baking sheet and roast in the preheated oven for about 25-30 minutes, or until tender. You can flip them cut-side up halfway through if you prefer a bit more caramelization.
2. **Prepare the Stuffing:**
   - While the squash is roasting, heat olive oil in a large skillet over medium heat.
   - Add the chopped onion and cook until softened, about 5 minutes.
   - Add the minced garlic and diced mushrooms (if using) and cook for another 3-4 minutes until the mushrooms are tender.
   - Stir in the chopped spinach or kale and cook until wilted.
   - Add the cooked quinoa, farro, or rice to the skillet along with the dried cranberries or raisins, chopped nuts, and cheese (if using). Mix well.
   - Season with dried thyme or rosemary, ground cumin (if using), salt, and black pepper. Cook for an additional 2-3 minutes to let the flavors combine.
3. **Stuff the Squash:**

- Remove the roasted squash from the oven and carefully flip them cut-side up.
- Spoon the stuffing mixture into each squash half, packing it in gently.
- Return the stuffed squash to the oven and bake for an additional 10-15 minutes, or until the stuffing is heated through and slightly golden on top.

4. **Serve:**
   - Remove from the oven and let cool slightly before serving.

This stuffed acorn squash makes a hearty and satisfying meal on its own, or it can be served as a side dish. It's perfect for a cozy dinner and can be customized with your favorite ingredients and flavors. Enjoy!

Harira Soup

Ingredients:

For the Soup:

- 2 tbsp olive oil
- 1 large onion, finely chopped
- 2 cloves garlic, minced
- 1 large celery stalk, finely chopped
- 1 large carrot, peeled and chopped
- 1 tsp ground ginger
- 1 tsp ground cinnamon
- 1/2 tsp ground turmeric
- 1/2 tsp ground cumin
- 1/2 tsp paprika
- 1/2 tsp ground black pepper
- 1/2 tsp cayenne pepper (optional, for heat)
- 1 can (14.5 oz/400 g) diced tomatoes, or 4-5 fresh tomatoes, peeled and chopped
- 1/2 cup dried lentils, rinsed
- 1/2 cup dried chickpeas, soaked overnight and drained (or 1 can chickpeas, drained and rinsed)
- 6 cups chicken or vegetable broth
- 1/4 cup fresh cilantro, chopped
- 1/4 cup fresh parsley, chopped
- Juice of 1 lemon
- 1/4 cup all-purpose flour (optional, for thickening)
- 1/4 cup water (if using flour)

For Garnish (optional):

- Fresh cilantro or parsley
- Lemon wedges

Instructions:

1. **Prepare the Vegetables:**
   - Heat olive oil in a large pot over medium heat.
   - Add the chopped onion, celery, and carrot. Cook until softened, about 5-7 minutes.
   - Stir in the minced garlic and cook for an additional minute.
2. **Add the Spices:**
   - Add the ground ginger, cinnamon, turmeric, cumin, paprika, black pepper, and cayenne pepper (if using). Stir to coat the vegetables with the spices and cook for 1-2 minutes until fragrant.

3. **Add the Tomatoes and Legumes:**
   - Stir in the diced tomatoes and cook for a few minutes.
   - Add the lentils, chickpeas, and broth. Bring the mixture to a boil.
4. **Simmer the Soup:**
   - Reduce the heat to low and let the soup simmer, partially covered, for about 30-40 minutes, or until the lentils and chickpeas are tender.
5. **Thicken the Soup (Optional):**
   - If you prefer a thicker soup, you can make a thickening mixture by combining 1/4 cup flour with 1/4 cup water to form a slurry. Stir this mixture into the soup and cook for an additional 5-10 minutes, until the soup has thickened.
6. **Add Fresh Herbs and Lemon Juice:**
   - Stir in the chopped cilantro and parsley.
   - Add the lemon juice and adjust seasoning with salt and pepper to taste.
7. **Serve:**
   - Ladle the soup into bowls and garnish with additional cilantro or parsley if desired. Serve with lemon wedges on the side.

Harira is a comforting, flavorful soup that's both filling and nutritious. It pairs well with crusty bread or flatbread for a complete meal. Enjoy your homemade Harira!

Spiced Lamb Chops

Ingredients:

For the Marinade:

- 8 lamb chops (rib or loin)
- 3 tbsp olive oil
- 3 cloves garlic, minced
- 1 tbsp fresh rosemary, finely chopped (or 1 tsp dried rosemary)
- 1 tbsp fresh thyme, finely chopped (or 1 tsp dried thyme)
- 1 tbsp ground cumin
- 1 tbsp ground paprika
- 1 tsp ground coriander
- 1/2 tsp ground cinnamon
- 1/2 tsp ground cayenne pepper (optional, for heat)
- 1 tbsp lemon juice
- Salt and black pepper to taste

Instructions:

1. **Prepare the Marinade:**
    - In a bowl, combine the olive oil, minced garlic, rosemary, thyme, cumin, paprika, coriander, cinnamon, cayenne pepper (if using), lemon juice, salt, and black pepper. Mix well to form a paste.
2. **Marinate the Lamb Chops:**
    - Pat the lamb chops dry with paper towels.
    - Rub the marinade all over the lamb chops, ensuring they are evenly coated.
    - Cover and refrigerate for at least 1 hour, or up to overnight for more intense flavor.
3. **Cook the Lamb Chops:**
Grilling:
    - Preheat your grill to medium-high heat.
    - Grill the lamb chops for about 4-5 minutes per side for medium-rare, or until they reach your desired level of doneness. The internal temperature should be 125°F (52°C) for medium-rare, 135°F (57°C) for medium, and 145°F (63°C) for medium-well.
4. **Pan-Seared:**
    - Heat a large skillet over medium-high heat with a little olive oil.
    - Add the lamb chops to the skillet and cook for about 4-5 minutes per side for medium-rare, or until they reach your desired level of doneness.
5. **Broiling:**
    - Preheat your oven's broiler and set the oven rack to the top position.

- Place the lamb chops on a broiler pan and broil for about 4-5 minutes per side for medium-rare, or until they reach your desired level of doneness.
6. **Rest and Serve:**
    - Transfer the cooked lamb chops to a plate and let them rest for about 5 minutes to allow the juices to redistribute.
    - Serve warm with your favorite sides, such as roasted vegetables, couscous, or a fresh salad.

Tips:

- For extra flavor, consider adding a touch of fresh mint to the marinade or as a garnish.
- Adjust the spices according to your taste preference. For example, add more cayenne for extra heat or reduce the cinnamon for a subtler flavor.

These spiced lamb chops are a delightful main course that pairs wonderfully with a variety of sides and sauces. Enjoy your meal!

Ingredients:

For the Marinade:

- 8 lamb chops (rib or loin)
- 3 tbsp olive oil
- 3 cloves garlic, minced
- 1 tbsp fresh rosemary, finely chopped (or 1 tsp dried rosemary)
- 1 tbsp fresh thyme, finely chopped (or 1 tsp dried thyme)
- 1 tbsp ground cumin
- 1 tbsp ground paprika
- 1 tsp ground coriander
- 1/2 tsp ground cinnamon
- 1/2 tsp ground cayenne pepper (optional, for heat)
- 1 tbsp lemon juice
- Salt and black pepper to taste

Instructions:

1. **Prepare the Marinade:**
    - In a bowl, combine the olive oil, minced garlic, rosemary, thyme, cumin, paprika, coriander, cinnamon, cayenne pepper (if using), lemon juice, salt, and black pepper. Mix well to form a paste.
2. **Marinate the Lamb Chops:**
    - Pat the lamb chops dry with paper towels.
    - Rub the marinade all over the lamb chops, ensuring they are evenly coated.
    - Cover and refrigerate for at least 1 hour, or up to overnight for more intense flavor.

3. **Cook the Lamb Chops:**
   Grilling:
   - Preheat your grill to medium-high heat.
   - Grill the lamb chops for about 4-5 minutes per side for medium-rare, or until they reach your desired level of doneness. The internal temperature should be 125°F (52°C) for medium-rare, 135°F (57°C) for medium, and 145°F (63°C) for medium-well.
4. **Pan-Seared:**
   - Heat a large skillet over medium-high heat with a little olive oil.
   - Add the lamb chops to the skillet and cook for about 4-5 minutes per side for medium-rare, or until they reach your desired level of doneness.
5. **Broiling:**
   - Preheat your oven's broiler and set the oven rack to the top position.
   - Place the lamb chops on a broiler pan and broil for about 4-5 minutes per side for medium-rare, or until they reach your desired level of doneness.
6. **Rest and Serve:**
   - Transfer the cooked lamb chops to a plate and let them rest for about 5 minutes to allow the juices to redistribute.
   - Serve warm with your favorite sides, such as roasted vegetables, couscous, or a fresh salad.

Tips:

- For extra flavor, consider adding a touch of fresh mint to the marinade or as a garnish.
- Adjust the spices according to your taste preference. For example, add more cayenne for extra heat or reduce the cinnamon for a subtler flavor.

These spiced lamb chops are a delightful main course that pairs wonderfully with a variety of sides and sauces. Enjoy your meal!

Eggplant and Chickpea Curry

Ingredients:

- 2 medium eggplants, cut into bite-sized cubes
- 1 can (15 oz/400 g) chickpeas, drained and rinsed
- 2 tbsp vegetable oil or olive oil
- 1 large onion, finely chopped
- 3 cloves garlic, minced
- 1 tbsp fresh ginger, minced
- 1 can (14.5 oz/400 g) diced tomatoes (or 2 cups fresh tomatoes, chopped)
- 1 cup coconut milk (optional for creaminess)
- 2 tsp ground cumin
- 1 tsp ground coriander
- 1 tsp ground turmeric
- 1 tsp ground paprika
- 1/2 tsp ground cinnamon
- 1/4 tsp ground cayenne pepper (optional, for heat)
- 1 tsp garam masala (optional, for extra flavor)
- Salt and black pepper to taste
- Fresh cilantro or parsley, chopped (for garnish)
- Juice of 1 lemon or lime (for finishing)

Instructions:

1. **Prepare the Eggplant:**
   - Heat 1 tablespoon of oil in a large skillet or pot over medium heat.
   - Add the eggplant cubes and cook, stirring occasionally, until they are golden brown and tender, about 8-10 minutes. You may need to do this in batches. Remove the eggplant from the skillet and set aside.
2. **Cook the Aromatics:**
   - In the same skillet, add the remaining tablespoon of oil.
   - Add the chopped onion and cook until softened and golden, about 5 minutes.
   - Stir in the minced garlic and ginger and cook for another 1-2 minutes, until fragrant.
3. **Add the Spices:**
   - Add the ground cumin, coriander, turmeric, paprika, cinnamon, and cayenne pepper (if using). Cook for 1 minute, stirring frequently, to toast the spices and enhance their flavors.
4. **Add Tomatoes and Chickpeas:**
   - Stir in the diced tomatoes and cook for about 5 minutes, until the tomatoes begin to break down and the sauce thickens slightly.
   - Add the chickpeas and coconut milk (if using). Stir well to combine.
5. **Simmer the Curry:**

- Return the cooked eggplant to the skillet and mix it into the sauce.
- Reduce the heat to low, cover, and let the curry simmer for about 15-20 minutes, until the flavors meld together and the sauce thickens. Stir occasionally to prevent sticking.

6. **Finish and Garnish:**
   - Season with salt and black pepper to taste.
   - Stir in the garam masala (if using) and lemon or lime juice.
   - Garnish with chopped fresh cilantro or parsley.

7. **Serve:**
   - Serve the curry hot over steamed rice, with naan bread, or with a side of yogurt.

Tips:

- For a richer flavor, you can use Greek yogurt or cream instead of coconut milk.
- Adjust the level of heat by varying the amount of cayenne pepper or adding a fresh chili if you like more spice.
- Feel free to add other vegetables like spinach, bell peppers, or potatoes to the curry for added variety.

This eggplant and chickpea curry is a flavorful and satisfying meal that's perfect for both weeknights and special occasions. Enjoy!

Lebanese Rice Pilaf

Ingredients:

- 1 cup long-grain rice (such as Basmati or Jasmine)
- 1/4 cup vermicelli noodles or broken spaghetti
- 2 tbsp olive oil or butter
- 1 small onion, finely chopped
- 2 cloves garlic, minced (optional)
- 2 cups chicken or vegetable broth
- 1/2 tsp ground cumin
- 1/2 tsp ground cinnamon
- 1/4 tsp ground black pepper
- Salt to taste
- 1/4 cup toasted pine nuts or almonds (optional, for garnish)
- Fresh parsley or cilantro, chopped (for garnish)

Instructions:

1. **Prepare the Rice:**
    - Rinse the rice under cold water until the water runs clear. This helps to remove excess starch and prevents the rice from becoming sticky. Drain well.
2. **Cook the Vermicelli:**
    - In a large saucepan or skillet, heat the olive oil or butter over medium heat.
    - Add the vermicelli noodles and cook, stirring frequently, until they turn golden brown. Be careful not to burn them.
3. **Sauté the Onion and Garlic:**
    - Add the finely chopped onion to the pan with the vermicelli and cook until softened and translucent, about 5 minutes.
    - If using garlic, add it now and cook for another minute, until fragrant.
4. **Add the Rice and Spices:**
    - Stir in the rinsed and drained rice, ground cumin, ground cinnamon, black pepper, and salt. Cook for 1-2 minutes, stirring frequently, to toast the rice slightly and coat it with the spices.
5. **Add the Broth:**
    - Pour in the chicken or vegetable broth and bring the mixture to a boil.
6. **Simmer:**
    - Reduce the heat to low, cover the pan, and let it simmer for about 18-20 minutes, or until the rice is cooked and the liquid is absorbed. Avoid lifting the lid while cooking to ensure the rice steams properly.
7. **Fluff the Rice:**
    - Once the rice is done, remove the pan from heat and let it sit, covered, for about 5 minutes.
    - Fluff the rice with a fork to separate the grains and incorporate the vermicelli.

8. **Garnish and Serve:**
    - Garnish with toasted pine nuts or almonds and chopped fresh parsley or cilantro if desired.
    - Serve warm alongside your favorite Middle Eastern dishes.

Tips:

- You can add other ingredients such as raisins or currants for a touch of sweetness, or sautéed vegetables for extra flavor.
- For a more robust flavor, use homemade broth instead of store-bought.

Lebanese rice pilaf is a versatile and tasty side dish that complements a variety of main courses, from grilled meats to stews. Enjoy!

Middle Eastern Chicken Stew

Ingredients:

- 2 lbs (900 g) chicken thighs or breasts, bone-in or boneless, cut into chunks
- 2 tbsp olive oil or vegetable oil
- 1 large onion, finely chopped
- 3 cloves garlic, minced
- 1 large carrot, peeled and chopped
- 1 large potato, peeled and chopped
- 1 bell pepper, chopped (optional)
- 1 can (14.5 oz/400 g) diced tomatoes
- 1 cup chicken broth
- 1/2 cup fresh lemon juice (about 2 lemons)
- 1 tsp ground cumin
- 1 tsp ground coriander
- 1/2 tsp ground turmeric
- 1/2 tsp ground paprika
- 1/2 tsp ground cinnamon
- 1/4 tsp ground black pepper
- 1/2 tsp ground cayenne pepper (optional, for heat)
- 1/2 tsp ground allspice (optional)
- 1/2 cup green olives, pitted and sliced (optional)
- Fresh cilantro or parsley, chopped (for garnish)
- Salt to taste

Instructions:

1. **Prepare the Chicken:**
   - Season the chicken pieces with salt and pepper.
2. **Brown the Chicken:**
   - In a large pot or Dutch oven, heat the olive oil over medium heat.
   - Add the chicken pieces and cook until browned on all sides, about 5-7 minutes. You may need to do this in batches. Remove the chicken from the pot and set aside.
3. **Sauté the Vegetables:**
   - In the same pot, add a little more oil if needed. Add the chopped onion and cook until softened and translucent, about 5 minutes.
   - Stir in the minced garlic and cook for an additional 1 minute until fragrant.
4. **Add Spices and Vegetables:**
   - Add the chopped carrot, potato, and bell pepper (if using) to the pot. Stir in the ground cumin, coriander, turmeric, paprika, cinnamon, black pepper, and cayenne pepper (if using). Cook for 2-3 minutes, stirring frequently, to toast the spices.

5. **Add Tomatoes and Broth:**
   - Stir in the diced tomatoes and chicken broth. Bring to a simmer.
6. **Simmer the Stew:**
   - Return the browned chicken to the pot. Cover and let the stew simmer over low heat for about 30-40 minutes, or until the chicken is cooked through and tender, and the vegetables are soft.
7. **Finish the Stew:**
   - Stir in the lemon juice and green olives (if using). Adjust seasoning with salt and pepper to taste.
   - Let the stew simmer for an additional 5 minutes to allow the flavors to meld.
8. **Garnish and Serve:**
   - Garnish with chopped fresh cilantro or parsley.
   - Serve the stew hot with steamed rice, couscous, or warm flatbread.

Tips:

- For extra flavor, consider marinating the chicken in a mixture of yogurt and spices before cooking.
- You can customize the stew by adding other vegetables like zucchini or bell peppers.
- If you prefer a thicker stew, you can mash some of the potatoes or carrots in the pot to thicken the broth.

This Middle Eastern chicken stew is both comforting and packed with flavor, making it a wonderful meal for any occasion. Enjoy!

Pita Bread with Za'atar

Ingredients:

- 4 pita breads
- 1/4 cup olive oil
- 2-3 tbsp za'atar spice blend (store-bought or homemade)
- 1/4 cup sesame seeds (optional, for extra crunch)
- Flaky sea salt (optional, for garnish)

Instructions:

1. **Preheat Oven:**
   - Preheat your oven to 375°F (190°C).
2. **Prepare the Pita Bread:**
   - Place the pita breads on a baking sheet. If they are large, you can cut them into halves or quarters to make smaller pieces.
3. **Brush with Olive Oil:**
   - Using a pastry brush or spoon, brush each pita bread generously with olive oil.
4. **Add Za'atar and Sesame Seeds:**
   - Sprinkle a liberal amount of za'atar spice blend over the oiled pita bread.
   - If using sesame seeds, sprinkle them on top as well.
5. **Bake:**
   - Place the baking sheet in the preheated oven and bake for about 10-12 minutes, or until the pita is crisp and golden brown. Keep an eye on it to prevent burning.
6. **Garnish (Optional):**
   - If desired, sprinkle a little flaky sea salt over the baked pita for extra flavor.
7. **Cool and Serve:**
   - Let the pita bread cool slightly before serving. It can be enjoyed warm or at room temperature.

Homemade Za'atar Spice Blend:

If you want to make your own za'atar blend, here's a simple recipe:

Ingredients:

- 2 tbsp dried thyme
- 2 tbsp dried oregano
- 2 tbsp sumac
- 1 tbsp sesame seeds
- 1/2 tsp salt
- 1/2 tsp ground cumin (optional)

Instructions:

1. Mix all the ingredients together in a bowl.
2. Store in an airtight container for up to 6 months.

Za'atar pita bread is perfect for dipping in hummus, enjoying with olives, or just eating on its own. It's a great addition to any Middle Eastern meal or a tasty snack for any time of day. Enjoy!

Tahini-Sesame Noodles

Ingredients:

- 8 oz (225 g) noodles (such as soba, rice noodles, or spaghetti)
- 1/4 cup tahini
- 2 tbsp soy sauce or tamari (for a gluten-free option)
- 1-2 tbsp honey or maple syrup (adjust to taste)
- 2 tbsp rice vinegar or white wine vinegar
- 1 tbsp sesame oil
- 2 cloves garlic, minced
- 1 tsp fresh ginger, grated (optional)
- 1/4 cup water (or more to adjust consistency)
- 1 tbsp toasted sesame seeds
- 1-2 scallions, sliced (for garnish)
- Fresh cilantro or parsley, chopped (for garnish)
- Red pepper flakes (optional, for a bit of heat)

Instructions:

1. **Cook the Noodles:**
   - Cook the noodles according to package instructions. Drain and rinse under cold water to stop the cooking process and prevent sticking.
2. **Prepare the Sauce:**
   - In a bowl, whisk together the tahini, soy sauce, honey (or maple syrup), rice vinegar, sesame oil, minced garlic, and grated ginger (if using). Add water a little at a time until the sauce reaches your desired consistency. It should be smooth and creamy but not too thick.
3. **Combine Noodles and Sauce:**
   - Toss the cooked noodles with the tahini sauce until well coated. If the noodles are too thick, add a bit more water to loosen the sauce.
4. **Garnish:**
   - Sprinkle toasted sesame seeds over the noodles.
   - Garnish with sliced scallions, chopped cilantro or parsley, and a pinch of red pepper flakes if you like a bit of heat.
5. **Serve:**
   - Serve the tahini-sesame noodles at room temperature or chilled. They make a great side dish or can be enjoyed as a light main course.

Tips:

- You can add vegetables such as shredded carrots, sliced bell peppers, or steamed broccoli to the noodles for added nutrition and texture.
- For extra protein, consider adding grilled chicken, tofu, or edamame.

- Adjust the sweetness and saltiness of the sauce according to your taste preferences.

Tahini-sesame noodles are not only quick to prepare but also packed with flavor. Enjoy this versatile dish as part of a larger meal or on its own!

Sweet and Savory Date Bars

Ingredients:

For the Bars:

- 1 1/2 cups pitted dates (about 12-15 dates)
- 1 cup raw nuts (such as almonds, walnuts, or pecans)
- 1/2 cup rolled oats
- 1/4 cup unsweetened shredded coconut (optional)
- 1/4 cup tahini or almond butter (for creaminess and binding)
- 1/4 cup honey or maple syrup
- 1/2 tsp ground cinnamon
- 1/4 tsp salt
- 1/4 tsp ground cardamom (optional, for extra flavor)
- 1/4 cup dark chocolate chips or chopped dark chocolate (optional, for a touch of indulgence)

For Topping (optional):

- Sea salt flakes
- Extra shredded coconut
- Chopped nuts

Instructions:

1. **Prepare the Dates:**
   - If the dates are dry or hard, soak them in warm water for about 10 minutes to soften. Drain well before using.
2. **Process the Ingredients:**
   - In a food processor, combine the pitted dates, raw nuts, rolled oats, and shredded coconut (if using). Pulse until the mixture is finely chopped and begins to stick together.
3. **Add the Bindings:**
   - Add the tahini (or almond butter), honey (or maple syrup), ground cinnamon, salt, and cardamom (if using). Process until the mixture is well combined and starts to form a sticky dough. You may need to scrape down the sides of the bowl a few times.
4. **Add Chocolate (Optional):**
   - If you're using chocolate chips, pulse them into the mixture briefly, just until evenly distributed.
5. **Press and Chill:**
   - Line an 8x8-inch (20x20 cm) baking pan with parchment paper or lightly grease it.

- Transfer the mixture into the pan and press it down firmly with your hands or a spatula to create an even layer.
6. **Add Toppings (Optional):**
    - Sprinkle a pinch of sea salt flakes, extra shredded coconut, or chopped nuts on top of the mixture, pressing them gently into the surface.
7. **Chill and Slice:**
    - Refrigerate the bars for at least 1-2 hours to firm up. Once set, lift the mixture out of the pan using the parchment paper and cut into squares or bars.
8. **Serve:**
    - Enjoy the date bars as a nutritious snack or a sweet treat.

Tips:

- Store the date bars in an airtight container in the refrigerator for up to 2 weeks. They can also be frozen for longer storage.
- For added flavor, consider mixing in dried fruits like cranberries or apricots, or adding a sprinkle of chia seeds or flaxseeds.

These sweet and savory date bars are not only delicious but also packed with energy and nutrients. They're perfect for a quick snack or a satisfying dessert!

www.ingramcontent.com/pod-product-compliance
Lightning Source LLC
LaVergne TN
LVHW081603060526
838201LV00054B/2059